IT HAPPENED IN VENICE

THE KINGSWOOD PLAYS FOR BOYS AND GIRLS

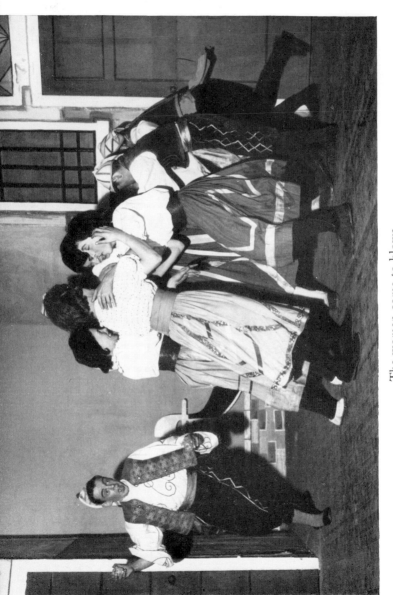

The women come to blows

A photograph of F. H. Davies' production at Pensby County Secondary School for boys, Heswall, Cheshire.

IT HAPPENED
IN VENICE

by

CARLO GOLDONI

A PLAY IN THREE ACTS

Translated and Adapted by
FREDERICK H. DAVIES

From the Carlo Signorelli Edition of
Le Baruffe Chiozzotte

HEINEMANN EDUCATIONAL
BOOKS LTD · LONDON

Heinemann Educational Books Ltd
LONDON MELBOURNE TORONTO
SINGAPORE CAPE TOWN
AUCKLAND IBADAN

First published by
Heinemann Educational Books Ltd 1965

Heinemann Educational Books Ltd
(Drama Department)
The Press at
Kingswood
Tadworth, Surrey

Published by Heinemann Educational Books Ltd
15–16 Queen Street, Mayfair, London W.1.
Printed in Great Britain by
Bookprint Limited, Kingswood, Surrey

INTRODUCTION

'Goldoni – good, gay, sunniest of souls, –
Glassing half Venice in that verse of thine, –
. . . Dear King of Comedy,
Be honoured! thou that didst love Venice so, –
Venice, and we who love her, all love thee!'

So wrote our English poet Robert Browning – who loved Venice, lived there for many years, and died there in his *palazzo* on the Grand Canal – when Carlo Goldoni's statue was unveiled.

If you wander down the busy Merceria, the 'Regent Street' of Venice, you will come to that statue. There he stands today, the man who wrote this and over a hundred other comedies, smiling quizzically down at the Venetians of the twentieth century.

Who was he, this Carlo Goldoni? He is so little known in our country. And yet to Italians he is what Shakespeare is to Englishmen. He is the *Gran Goldoni*. And to the children of Venice, as to their fathers and mothers, he is still *papà Goldoni*.

He was born in Venice on 25 February 1707. He died in Paris during the French Revolution, on 6 February 1793, only a few days after Louis XVI was taken to the guillotine. For forty-six of those eighty-six years of his life, Carlo Goldoni was ceaselessly writing plays for the theatres of Italy and France. During one of these years, in order to save the

theatre in Venice for which he was working from having to
close down, he made a rash promise that he would write
sixteen plays in one year. He wrote afterwards in his Memoirs:
'It was a terrible year for me, which I cannot recall without
trembling.'

The wonder is that Goldoni did not die in his attempt to
keep that rash promise. For keep it he did. He had set himself
the stupendous physical task of writing the equivalent of five
modern novels in one year. How he kept that promise is best
told by Goldoni himself:

Only one play remained to be written to fulfil my promise
to my Venetian public. We had reached the last Sunday but
one of the season and I had not written a single line of the
sixteenth play. I left my house for a walk about St Mark's
Square. I kept looking about for something – anything –
which might supply me with a subject for the sixteenth
play. Then, under the arcade of the clock-tower, I saw him,
the man who was to provide me with the subject I was
looking for. He was an old, dirty, poorly dressed Armenian
who went about the streets of Venice selling dried fruit
which he called *abagigi*. This man was so well known and
so much laughed at, that when anyone wanted to tease a
girl looking for a husband, they suggested she should
marry Abagigi.

I needed no more. I went back to my house, shut myself
up in my room, and began the comedy which I called *The
Women's Gossip*. With it we closed the season. The audience
was so large that we had to double and treble the price of
the boxes, and the applause was so long and loud that
passers-by wondered whether a riot was taking place. I sat
quietly in my box. Then crowds of people came and
dragged me out and began paying me compliments which
I would have been glad to have avoided.

I was tired and really a little vexed that they should seem to be placing this play so much higher than others which I had written and thought better. Gradually, however, the truth dawned upon me: they were really acclaiming the triumph of my having kept my promise, of having done what I had said I would do.

In the short space of this introduction it is not possible to tell you nearly as much as I should like to about Carlo Goldoni. This incident will perhaps have given you some idea of the sort of man he was. He achieved fame through facing and overcoming many, many difficulties; and yet he remained to the end of his long and hard life one of the most lovable and courageous of men. In his Memoirs he tells us of the happy day, when, as a young man, he brought his lovely bride home to Venice. When he died in Paris, old, in poverty, and blind in one eye, that bride was still at his side, his deeply devoted wife to the very end of his long life.

TO THE PRODUCER

The following suggestions, arising from a most successful and enjoyable production of this play with twelve- to fifteen-year-old secondary modern boys, may be found of value.

The play will probably require a little longer, or a little more intensive, period of rehearsals than is usually given to school plays, since its successful production depends upon a certain pace being attained.

Many of the lines are so short – giving the effect of quick repartee – that I found it better to discourage the learning of lines until well over half-way through rehearsals. By doing this, the boys gradually, and without realizing it, memorized the movements and lines together. For when they were at last told that they must do without their scripts by a certain date, they found that they practically knew their parts already through constant repetition.

Timing of cues and 'pointing' of words assume, of course, a greater importance in a fast comedy like this. The relation of the timing of cues to the obtaining of necessary pace is often completely misunderstood by boys, and they constantly had to be reminded at first that pace is *not* obtained by gabbling their lines quickly but simply by being very quick on their cues.

The squabbles between the women, and the stone-throwing scene, need to be very carefully rehearsed. To leave these to the improvisation of young actors is to invite disaster. Each actor must know the exact timing of his every movement so that when the fight or the brawl ends each will find himself in his correct position to continue the action of the play.

The stones thrown by TOFFOLO may be made out of papier-mâché, about two to three inches in diameter, and painted grey and white. If the stone which should hit CAPTAIN TONI on the shoulder misses him, he should still clutch his shoulder with his hand, and owing to the speed of the action the miss will go unnoticed by the audience.

The lace-frames may be made out of plywood, about 8″ by 12″. The shuttles, 3″ long and 1″ wide, were made of metal.

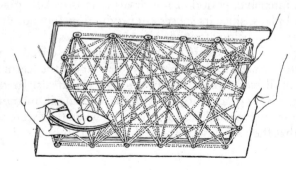

The thread (white wool) should have been woven from the shuttle across the frame from drawing pins to make it easier for the actors during performances.

In order not to distract the attention of the audience from the actors, pale pinks, greys and blues were used for the scenery. On the other hand, the costumes were hired from those actually used in Gilbert and Sullivan's *The Gondoliers* – all very gay and colourful. The wigs worn by the women should be as contrasted from each other as possible: LUCIETTA preferably having red hair and CHECCA black hair.

Interval music between the Acts could be of the Santa Lucia type, but during the quick changes between scenes (and these were accomplished with a speed which astonished the audience), very fast and gay piano music was considered essential, e.g. the sparkling, tarantella-like *Presto con fuoco* with which Beethoven ends his Piano Sonata No. 18 (Op. 31, No. 3).

Any attempt to supply 'Notes on the Characters' would be superfluous: a first reading of the play will reveal their widely differing types and temperaments. The part of FORTUNATO, however, may be made even more amusing if in addition to his stutter he can acquire a slight nervous twitch of head and arms.

All stage directions are from the point of view of the actors and not of the audience.

TO THE AUDIENCE
(Suggested Programme Note)

This play won the praise of both Goethe and Voltaire. It has been performed in Italy more times than any other of Goldoni's plays.

It has a very simple and very human plot – a quarrel between two Venetian fishing families. When the curtain rises the men are still away at sea. Their women-folk, seated at their lace-frames, are eagerly looking forward to their return, because LUCIETTA is expecting to become engaged to TITTA-NANE and ORSETTA to BEPPE.

At large in the streets of Venice, however, is TOFFOLO (nicknamed 'Monkey-face'), a lazy young boatman who thinks himself quite a lad with the ladies.

When this young fellow, strolling down the street, sees pretty LUCIETTA lace-making, he buys her a roasted sweetmeat from a passing street-vendor. But when he offers to treat CHECCA, she refuses, piqued at not being invited first. Aspersions are cast between LUCIETTA and CHECCA, which start the fiery ball of Italian temper rolling.

A veritable storm in a teacup bursts when the men return, for LUCIETTA cattishly whispers to her brother BEPPE to beware of TOFFOLO'S attentions to ORSETTA, while CHECCA, with equal cattiness, informs TITTA-NANE that TOFFOLO has given LUCIETTA a roasted sweetmeat. With their knives drawn, BEPPE and TITTA-NANE set off in search of TOFFOLO.

But we need not fear; in the plays of Goldoni nobody dies. The women intervene, and TOFFOLO, shaken and shouting revenge, is left unharmed. He lodges an exaggerated complaint and the Commissioner sends a sergeant to fetch both the families for questioning at the Chancellery. Sheer comedy follows and the Commissioner closes his enquiry in frantic desperation, convinced that there is some plot to drive him mad.

His benevolent nature, however, forces him to try to patch up the quarrel, and in the third act he eventually succeeds in reconciling the embroiled couples, LUCIETTA with TITTA-

NANE, ORSETTA with BEPPE, and CHECCA with TOFFOLO.

Among all Goldoni's comedies, there is none so pulsating with life. It is a frolic – light, superficial, exaggerated; but, at the same time, a brilliant frolic, glittering and sparkling, full of charm and gaiety.

F.H.D.

THE PLAYERS IN ORDER
OF APPEARANCE

LUCIETTA (Lootchee*ayt*-ta), Captain Toni's sister

PASQUA (*Pas*kwa), Captain Toni's wife

LIBERA (Leeb*ay*ra), Fortunato's wife

ORSETTA (Ors*ayt*-ta), Libera's sister

CHECCA (*Kay*k-ka), Libera's younger sister

TOFFOLO (*Toff*oloh), a young boatman, the local dandy

CANNOCHIO (Cann*ok*ioh), a seller of roasted sweetmeats

VINCENZO (Vin*tchen*tso), a retired fisherman

CAPTAIN TONI, owner of a fishing-boat

BEPPE (Bayp-pay), Toni's brother, engaged to Orsetta

FORTUNATO (Forrrtoon*at*oh), a fisherman who stutters

TITTA-NANE (*Tee*tah-*Nah*nay), a fisherman engaged to Lucietta

ISIDORO (Iz*ee*doroh), Commissioner of Police

SERGEANT OF POLICE

SANSUGA   } (San*soo*ga) servants to Isidoro
SANSOVINO } (Sanso*vee*no)

ACT I: MORNING

ACT II: AFTERNOON

ACT III: EARLY EVENING

ACT I

Scene I

The scene is a street in Venice in the mid-eighteenth century. Left and right are the fronts of the houses. Backstage is the canal. PASQUA *and* LUCIETTA *are seated in front of their house on the right.* LIBERA, ORSETTA *and* CHECCA *are seated on another bench in front of their house, left. All are busy making lace on frames.*[1] *The time is early morning.*

LUCIETTA: I suppose you all realize that they've been away over a week now. Oh, dear, I do hope the weather won't change.

ORSETTA: So do I. What way is the wind blowing, Lucietta?

LUCIETTA: Heavens, don't ask me! (*To* PASQUA.) Sister-in-law, which way is the wind blowing?

PASQUA: You engaged to be married to a fisherman, and you can't tell the sirocco yet?

LUCIETTA: Is that good? Will it bring them in quicker?

PASQUA: Of course it will, you ninny. Our men are in luck's way.

LIBERA: You're right, Pasqua. We might even have them back today.

CHECCA: Oh dear, I'd better hurry. I wanted to have this lace finished before they got back.

LUCIETTA: Why, how much have you still to do, Checca?

[1] see Introduction: Note to the Producer

CHECCA: Nearly an arm's length, I should say.

LIBERA: You work too slowly, my girl.

CHECCA (*calling across to* PASQUA): Donna Pasqua! My brother-in-law, Fortunato, is on your husband's boat, isn't he?

LIBERA: Get on with your work and don't ask silly questions. You know very well my husband is with Captain Toni.

CHECCA: And with Beppe? Pasqua, Captain Toni's brother, *is* with him as well, isn't he?

PASQUA: Of course. They always sail together, now that Beppe's old enough.

CHECCA: And Titta-Nane? Is *he* with your husband as well?

LUCIETTA (*quickly to* CHECCA): Of course! Why do you ask that? What do you want with Titta-Nane?

CHECCA: Me? Nothing!

LUCIETTA: You know quite well Titta-Nane has been walking out with me for two years now. *And* that he's promised to give me the engagement ring as soon as they get back.

CHECCA (*aside*): What a cat! She wants them all for herself.

ORSETTA (*to* LUCIETTA): Don't be so touchy, Lucietta! Checca can't get married until after I do. Your brother, Beppe, and I will be getting engaged as soon as they get back, as well as you and Titta-Nane. There will be plenty of time for my little sister here.

CHECCA (*to* LIBERA): I suppose you'd all be very happy if I never get married.

LIBERA: Hold your tongue and get on with your work.

CHECCA (*aside*): I'll get married all right. And my husband won't leave *me* on my own to go off fishing for crabs!

TOFFOLO, *the local dandy, an idle good-for-nothing, enters back stage and comes jauntily down to beside* LUCIETTA.

LUCIETTA: Good morning, Toffolo!

TOFFOLO: And a very good morning to you, Lucietta!
He stands near LUCIETTA, *ogling her flirtatiously and ignoring the others.*

ORSETTA: Hey, gormless, we're here as well.

TOFFOLO: Patience, girls. You must all take your turn!

CHECCA (*aside*): Toffolo, for instance, would suit me fine.

PASQUA: What's the matter, young man? No work to do, today?

TOFFOLO: I've just finished. There was only a cargo of vegetables to fetch from the docks.

LUCIETTA: Didn't they pay you?

TOFFOLO: Sure! I'm rolling in it. Anything you fancy, just say the word.

CHECCA (*to* ORSETTA): Did you ever hear anything like it? She's just leading him on!

TOFFOLO (*to* LUCIETTA): Don't go away. (*He goes right and calls off stage.*) Hey, you! You – with the roasted sweetmeats!

CANOCCHIO (*entering right carrying a flat basket, suspended from his shoulders, in front of him*): Yes, sir. What would you like, sir?

TOFFOLO: Let's see what you've got. Bring them over here. (*He goes back to* LUCIETTA, *followed by* CANOCCHIO.)

CANOCCHIO: Take your pick, sir. Everything just straight from the oven.

TOFFOLO: Will you have a sweetmeat, Lucietta?

LUCIETTA: Thank you kindly, sir, she said! I'll have – that one!

TOFFOLO: What about you, Pasqua? Would you like one?

PASQUA: I certainly would. If there's one thing I could never refuse, it's a sweetmeat. Give me one of those, young man.

TOFFOLO: That's the spirit! Sweetmeats for sweet ladies, eh? But aren't you going to eat yours, Lucietta?

LUCIETTA: It's hot. I'll wait till it cools down a little.

CHECCA (*calling across to* CANOCCHIO): Hi! You, young man! Come over here.

CANOCCHIO(*going across to her*): Here I am.

CHECCA: What can I have for half a soldini?

TOFFOLO(*crossing to* CHECCA): Allow me! This is on me.

CHECCA: Not with me it isn't.

TOFFOLO: But why ever not?

CHECCA: Because I'm not one of *your* sweet ladies.

LUCIETTA (*to* PASQUA, *but loud enough for* CHECCA *to hear*): Listen to Miss Hoity-toity! Just because she wasn't offered one first.

CHECCA (*calling across to* LUCIETTA): Don't you go trying to start a quarrel! It's simply that *I'm* not the sort of girl who goes round accepting things from every Tom, Dick and Harry.

LUCIETTA: Meaning that I do?

CHECCA: Well, you did take those shell-fish that old Fosco's son gave you.

LUCIETTA: Me? Liar!

PASQUA(*to* LUCIETTA): That's enough!

LIBERA (*to* CHECCA): Stop it, both of you!

CANOCCHIO: Anybody want another one?

TOFFOLO: No. That 'll be all, thank you.

CANOCCHIO (*as he goes*): Sweetmeats! Fresh-roasted sweet-meats! Come and get your sweetmeats! (*Exit.*)

> *The women go on with their lace-making.* TOFFOLO *wanders down behind* LIBERA, ORSETTA *and* CHECCA. *As he passes* CHECCA, *who is sitting at the end of the bench, he taps her on the shoulder and beckons her down left. She puts her lace-frame on the bench and follows him.*

TOFFOLO (*aside*): I'll have to try and remember that you don't seem to like me!

CHECCA (*turning to go back to her lace*): Oh, go away! I'm busy.

TOFFOLO (*aside*): Well, if that's really how you feel, I suppose I'd better not tell you about my boat.

CHECCA (*stops midway and then comes back to him down left*): What boat?

TOFFOLO (*aside*): My god-father's going to buy me a boat and when I've made enough money at the ferry, I'll be thinking of marrying.

CHECCA (*aside*): D'you really mean it?

TOFFOLO (*aside*): So it's a pity you don't seem to like me.

CHECCA (*aside*): Oh, it wasn't you I meant, really. It was the sweetmeats.

LIBERA (*aloud to* TOFFOLO): Tell me, do you never stop blathering?

TOFFOLO: All right, I'm going. (*He walks back behind them.* CHECCA *returns to her seat.*)

LIBERA: Well, hurry up about it.

TOFFOLO: What've I done wrong now? All right, all right! I said I was going. (*He walks back stage, pretending unconcern, and then comes cautiously down right stage to* LUCIETTA *and* PASQUA.)

LUCIETTA (*to* PASQUA): Did you ever hear anything like it? Putting on airs at her age!

PASQUA (*to* LUCIETTA): Yes, if you only knew how she exasperates me!

TOFFOLO (*approaching from back stage ingratiatingly*): You certainly do work quickly, Donna Pasqua.

PASQUA: Oh, this is only some cheap lace – only worth ten soldi.

TOFFOLO: And yours, Lucietta?

LUCIETTA: Oh, mine's worth thirty soldi!

TOFFOLO: Yes, it *is* beautiful, isn't it?

LUCIETTA: You like it?

TOFFOLO: Yeh, I think it's smashing. It's all so small, so finely worked.

LUCIETTA (*making room for him on the bench*): Come nearer – and look at it closer.

TOFFOLO (*sitting between* LUCIETTA *and* PASQUA): A thorn between two roses, eh? (*He laughs loudly at his joke.*)

CHECCA (*nudging* ORSETTA, *indicating to her* TOFFOLO *close to* LUCIETTA): Just look at that!

ORSETTA: Take no notice. Don't upset yourself.

TOFFOLO (*to* LUCIETTA): Isn't anybody *here* going to tell me to go away?

LUCIETTA: You are a one! Why should we send you away?

ORSETTA (*pointing to* LUCIETTA *opposite: to* LIBERA): What d'you make of that?

TOFFOLO (*affectedly*): Donna Pasqua, will you partake of a little snuff?

PASQUA: Is it good snuff?

TOFFOLO: The best! From Malamocco.

PASQUA: Give me a pinch of it, then.

CHECCA (*aside to* ORSETTA): If only poor Titta-Nane could see her now!

TOFFOLO: And you, Lucietta, will you partake?

LUCIETTA: Yes, I will. Just to annoy *her* over there. (*She jerks her thumb towards* CHECCA.)

TOFFOLO: Who? Little sour-puss?

CHECCA (*aside*): I wonder if they're talking about me?

LUCIETTA: But I thought you liked her?

TOFFOLO: What gave you that idea?

LUCIETTA (*laughing*): Do you know what we call her? Sheep-face!

TOFFOLO: Sheep-face?

LUCIETTA: Yes! You know! Because she's always making sheep's eyes at the men! (TOFFOLO *laughs loudly*.)

CHECCA (*calling across to them*): Can't we all share the joke? TOFFOLO *takes no notice but nudges* LUCIETTA *and loudly imitates a sheep.*

TOFFOLO: Mmmmaaa! Mmmmaaaa!

As each of the women in turn now rises, each puts her lace-frame on the bench behind her.

CHECCA (*rising*): Just what's that supposed to mean?

ORSETTA (*rising, to* CHECCA): Don't take any notice!

LIBERA (*rising, to* CHECCA *and* ORSETTA): Get on with your work, both of you.

ORSETTA: You'd do better to make fun of yourself, Mister Monkey-face!

TOFFOLO (*rising*): What's that you called me?

ORSETTA: Don't pretend you don't know. Everybody calls you Monkey-face!

LUCIETTA (*rising*): *You* needn't talk! What about yourself!

ORSETTA (*taking a step centre*): You keep your tongue out of this, Miss Tittle-tattle!

LUCIETTA (*step centre*): Ha! Just listen to old pasty-face.

LIBERA (*going up to* LUCIETTA): How dare you call my sisters names like that!

PASQUA (*rising and pushing herself between* LUCIETTA *and* LIBERA): And you'd better be careful how you speak to *my* sister!

LIBERA: Oh, you pipe down, old fish-face.

PASQUA: Pipe down yourself, you old shrew!

TOFFOLO (*moving away down right*): Gor! A rose between two thorns, more like it!

LIBERA: Oh! Just you wait till my husband gets back!

CHECCA: Yes, and you just wait until Titta-Nane gets back. I'll tell him everything. Yes – everything!

PASQUA   Just you wait till Captain Toni gets back!

LIBERA   Fortunato is not afraid of your husband!

    (*together*):

ORSETTA Yes, there'll be trouble all right for you when Fortunato comes home!

LUCIETTA When Captain Toni hears about this you'll be sorry!

  VINCENZO *enters right in the middle of the hubbub and shouts.*

VINCENZO (*shouting*): Ladies! Ladies! *Quiet!!* What on earth's the matter with youse all?

LUCIETTA (*going to* VINCENZO): Oh, Vincenzo, if you could have heard the names they've been . . .

CHECCA (*coming centre*): That's right, Vincenzo, you listen to Miss Tittle-tattle here and . . .

VINCENZO (*crossing to down left*): Calm yourselves, ladies! Captain Toni's fishing smack's just coming in!

PASQUA (*aside to* LUCIETTA): Don't say any more!

LIBERA (*aside to* CHECCA *and* ORSETTA): For heaven's sake don't tell Fortunato anything about all this!

ORSETTA: Beppe mustn't know, either!

TOFFOLO (*to* LUCIETTA): You needn't be frightened. I'll stick up for you.

LUCIETTA: Oh, go away, you!

PASQUA: Yes, just leave us alone, will you?

TOFFOLO: That settles it! I shall go back to Checca!

  He crosses right to CHECCA *and her sisters and is rejected by them also.*

LIBERA   Be off with you!

ORSETTA (*to* TOFFOLO): Hop it, you!

CHECCA   Go to the devil!

TOFFOLO (*turning indignantly to* VINCENZO *down left*): Did

you ever see such women! To speak to me like that!
Telling *me* to go to the devil!

VINCENZO: Try drowning yourself. (*He crosses in front of*
TOFFOLO *to speak to* LIBERA.)

TOFFOLO (*pulling* VINCENZO *around by the shoulder*): And
just what d'you think *you* mean by that?

VINCENZO (*giving him a cuff which sends him staggering*): Stop
shoving yer spoke in when yer elders is waiting to speak!

TOFFOLO (*backing away from* VINCENZO): I'm sorry – I
didn't mean to. Sorry, I'm sure. (*Exit left hastily.*)

PASQUA (*crossing to* VINCENZO): Have our husbands landed
yet?

VINCENZO: They've moored the boat along the Zattere.
I'm just going along there meself to see if I can get any fish
from them to sell at my shop.

LIBERA: Oh, Vincenzo, you won't *say* anything to them,
will you?

VINCENZO: Say anything?

PASQUA: You won't go and tell them about the little tiff
we've been having?

VINCENZO: What d'yer take me for? (*Exit left.*)

LIBERA (*to* PASQUA): It would be a fine how d'you do if our
men found us all quarrelling on their first day home.

PASQUA (*to* LIBERA): You should know me by now. I'm
quick-tempered but I soon get over it.

LUCIETTA: Are you still annoyed, Checca?

CHECCA: Are you still going to try to annoy me?

ORSETTA: That's enough, Checca. Let's be friends again,
Lucietta?

LUCIETTA: Why not?

ORSETTA: And you, as well, Checca!

CHECCA: I wouldn't lower myself!

LUCIETTA: Oh, don't be such a ninny!

CHECCA: Oh, well, all right – but don't you start trying to be funny again, or it'll be the worse for you.

PASQUA: Lucietta, bring your frame in and we'll go along and meet them. (*She goes into her house right, carrying her lace-frame.*)

LIBERA (*to* CHECCA *and* ORSETTA): Bring yours in as well, and we'll go and meet them, too. (*She goes into her house left, carrying her lace-frame.*)

ORSETTA (*taking up her frame*): I can't wait to see my Beppe again! (*Exit into house left.*)

CHECCA (*to* LUCIETTA): Remember – be nicer to me and no more of your funny remarks! (*Goes into house, left, carrying her lace-frame.*)

LUCIETTA (*calling after as she goes into house, right, with her frame*): Don't worry – I'll do my best!

Quick CURTAIN

Scene II

The quay. This short scene can be played with the permanent set hidden either by a drop curtain, suitably painted, or simply by the tabs. CAPTAIN TONI *is standing right centre speaking to* FORTUNATO, BEPPE *and* TITTA-NANE *who are still on the fishing smack off stage right.*

TONI: That's right, boys! Gently does it, now! Careful, Beppe, with that large basket. It's been hard work catching those fish!

   VINCENZO *enters left.*

VINCENZO: Welcome 'ome, Captain Toni!

TONI (*turning slightly*): Ah, it's you, old Vincenzo! Yes, it's good to be back.

VINCENZO: Everything go all right, eh?

TONI (*facing right again to watch his men unloading off right*): Nothing to complain of.

VINCENZO: And what have yer got for us this time?

TONI: Oh, a bit of everything.

VINCENZO: Can yer let me 'ave four baskets of sole?

TONI: Probably.

VINCENZO: And can yer let me 'ave four baskets of mullet?

TONI: I think so.

VINCENZO: What's the mullet like, eh? Big uns?

TONI: Big ones? Of course they are! Big as ox tongues!

VINCENZO: Yer wouldn't have any turbot, as well, would yer?

TONI: I'll say we have! As big as the bottom of a barrel!

VINCENZO: D'yer think I could – er – have a look at 'em?

TONI: Go ahead. You'd better hurry aboard before Fortunato shares it out.

VINCENZO (*going right*): Good! Good! Yer' splendid chaps to deal with, you fishermen! (*Exit.*)

TONI (*alone*): It'll be a bit of luck if I can get *him* to take the whole catch.

   BEPPE *enters right carrying a basket of fish.*

BEPPE: I say! Brother!

TONI: Yes, what is it, Beppe?

BEPPE: If you're agreeable, I'd like to send this basket of brill to the Commissioner.

TONI: What on *earth* d'you want to do that for?

BEPPE: Well, you know he's going to be the witness at my wedding.

TONI: If you've really made up your mind about that, you can give him them with pleasure. But don't kid yourself

that he'll ever lift *his* little finger to help you, just because
he was the witness of your marriage, and because you sent
him a basket of brill.

> PASQUA *and* LUCIETTA *enter left.* BEPPE *puts basket on
> floor.*

PASQUA: Toni!

TONI: Pasqua!

LUCIETTA (*to* TONI): Welcome back, brother!

TONI: Hello, Lucietta!

LUCIETTA (*to* BEPPE): And you, little brother, welcome
back also!

BEPPE: How's things with you, sister?

LUCIETTA: Oh, fine! How's yourself?

BEPPE: Fine, fine! (*To* PASQUA.) And you, sister-in-law,
how've you been keeping?

PASQUA: Very well, thank you, Beppe. (*To* TONI.) Have
you had a good voyage?

TONI: Ay, ay! Let's not talk of that! We've brought back
the fish, and here we all are safe and sound again!

LUCIETTA: Did you get me anything?

TONI: One fine silk handkerchief and two pairs of scarlet
stockings!

LUCIETTA: Oh, what a wonderful brother! He is good,
isn't he, Pasqua?

PASQUA: That depends on what he's brought for me.

TONI: For you, wife, I've brought something you'll be able
to make a petticoat and a skirt out of.

PASQUA: What colour is it?

TONI: You'll see.

PASQUA: But I want to know what colour it is!

TONI: And I've told you – you'll wait and see!

LUCIETTA (*to* BEPPE): Haven't *you* brought me anything,
Beppe?

BEPPE: Oh, come now, sister! Did you really expect me to get you anything? (*Moves down left.*) As a matter of fact, I've bought the engagement ring for Orsetta!

LUCIETTA(*following him eagerly down left*): Oh, do let's see it! Is it a nice one?

BEPPE(*showing her the ring*): There it is!

LUCIETTA: Oh, it's beautiful! And to think it's for that woman!

BEPPE: That woman! What way's that to speak of Orsetta?

LUCIETTA: Well, if you only knew what she's been up to! Ask our sister-in-law, here. (*She crosses to beside* PASQUA *down left.*)

PASQUA: And Donna Libera! Don't forget her!

TONI (*moving forward centre*): What *is* this? What's been happening?

BEPPE (*moving in left centre*): Yes, just what *is* all this about?

LUCIETTA: Oh, nothing! Just their wicked tongues, that's all. They ought to have them pulled out with red-hot pincers.

PASQUA: Yes, indeed! *There* we were, on our own doorstep, minding our own business, working away on our lace-frames . . .

LUCIETTA: We weren't even taking any notice of *them* at all . . .

PASQUA: And all because of that little scoundrel Monkey-face Toffolo!

LUCIETTA: Just fancy being jealous of that little namby-pamby!

BEPPE: What? *You* mean Orsetta has been *speaking* to Monkey-face Toffolo?

LUCIETTA: Oh, yes, she was speaking to him all right!

TONI: That's enough! Stop provoking the lad and starting more trouble!

PASQUA: Yes, that's enough, Lucietta. Or else everybody'll be putting the blame on us.

BEPPE: Look, just exactly who was Monkey-face speaking to?

LUCIETTA: Oh, everybody.

BEPPE: Has – he – been – speaking to Orsetta?

LUCIETTA (*looking at* PASQUA): It – it seemed to me – that he was.

BEPPE: The devil he was!

TONI: I said that's enough! Let us go – or I'll be getting annoyed, myself!

BEPPE: Well, that finishes it with me – as far as Orsetta's concerned – and as for that Monkey-face – by Heavens, I'll make him pay for this – won't I just?

TONI: *Are* we going home, or *aren't* we?

LUCIETTA: But what about Titta-Nane? Where is Titta-Nane?

TONI: As far as I know – or care – he's still on the boat.

LUCIETTA: I *would* like to tell him I'm glad you're all back safely.

TONI: I've told you – I'm waiting to go home!

LUCIETTA: Why? What's the hurry?

TONI: You've all done enough tittle-tattling for today!

LUCIETTA: You see, sister-in-law? Didn't we say we'd best keep our mouths shut?

PASQUA (*advancing on* TONI *and shaking her finger under his nose*): Tittle-tattling, indeed! Well, who began it, eh? Just tell me that! Who began tittle-tattling?

LUCIETTA: Yes, I'd like to know what it is that I've said!

PASQUA: And me! Nobody can say that *I've* opened my mouth much.

BEPPE (*shouting*): You've both opened your mouths so much

that if Orsetta came along now all she'd get would be a
thump on the snout! (*He picks up his basket of fish.*)

LUCIETTA: But . . .

BEPPE (*bellowing*): I don't want to hear any more! I'll go and
sell the ring right away! (*He starts going left.*)

LUCIETTA (*running after him*): Oh, no, Beppe! I'd like it! Let
me have it!

BEPPE (*shouting still louder*): If you don't shut up, I'll let you
have something you won't like. (*Exit left.*)

TONI (*to* LUCIETTA): And it'd only be what you deserve!
Now, let us go *home*! Everybody! Immediately!

LUCIETTA (*moving front left*): What fine manners we've got!
Just *who* d'you think *you're* talking to? Your servant? Oh,
don't worry! Don't think I've got to stay with you. As
soon as I see Titta-Nane, I'll tell him everything. And if he
won't marry me right away, I – I'll get a job as a maid-
servant! (*Exit left.*)

PASQUA: Now, see what you've done!

TONI (*making as if to box her ears*): Would you like to bet that
in a moment I won't . . .

PASQUA (*to* TONI): That's right! Start raising your arm
again and you haven't been home five minutes. Men! They
make me sick! (*Exit after* LUCIETTA.)

TONI (*following and calling after her*): What about you, eh?
What about you? Women! They're no better than crabs –
fit only for baiting traps! (*Exit left.*)

   TITTA-NANE *and* VINCENZO *enter right, having evidently
   overheard the last remarks of* PASQUA *and* TONI.

TITTA-NANE: Now what could all that hubbub've been
about?

VINCENZO: Ah, Donna Pasqua gets up in the air about
nothing. You know her.

TITTA-NANE: Yes, but Lucietta's gone as well. And she

knew I couldn't get down to see her till all the fish were landed.

VINCENZO (*centre stage*): You was scared to see her, more like, if you ask me.

TITTA-NANE (*turning back to him*): A lot you know about it.
FORTUNATO *follows them on – right.*

FORTUNATO (*who stutters*): – 'incenzo!

VINCENZO: Yes, what is it, Fortunato?

FORTUNATO: Your f-fish is all ready for you. F-four b-b-b-baskets of sole, two b-b-b-baskets of mullet, and six of t-t-t-turbot.

VINCENZO: And six of what?

FORTUNATO: And six of t-t-t-t-turbot!

VINCENZO: I can't make out what you say.

FORTUNATO: You can't make out what I say? Four b-b-baskets of sole, two of m-m-mullet, and six of t-t-t-turbot!

VINCENZO (*aside to* TITTA-NANE): He's a card, this one! I could listen to 'im all day.

FORTUNATO: You'll have t-t-t-to send for them! But I'll c-c-come for the money myself.

VINCENZO: Certainly! Any time will do fine! I'll have it all ready for you.

FORTUNATO: P-p-p-pinch 'v snuff?

VINCENZO: Come again?

FORTUNATO: Snuff! Snuff!

VINCENZO: Ah! Compris! Capito! A pinch of snuff! (*Takes out his snuff-box, opens it, and proffers it to* FORTUNATO.) Help yerself, lad.

FORTUNATO (*taking a pinch*): I d-d-d-dropped my own over b-b-b-b- – into the sea. I c-c-c-could've bought some in Senagaglia, b-b-but theirs isn't as g-g-good as ours. (*Sniffs.*) This is g-g-good!

VINCENZO (*nudging* TITTA-NANE): What was that? I still can't quite make out what you say!

FORTUNATO (*shouting*): Good! Good! Good! Do I speak f-foreign language? Eh? Or do I speak our language? Yes or no?

VINCENZO: Sure! Compris! Capito! Well, I must be getting along now. Thanks for letting me have the fish, Titta-Nane. I'll have the money ready for you, Fortunato. (*Exit left.*)

TITTA-NANE: You coming now, Fortunato?

FORTUNATO: W-w-w-wait!

TITTA-NANE: What's there to wait for now?

FORTUNATO: W-w-w-wait!

TITTA-NANE: W-w-w-wait? *For* what?

FORTUNATO: I must g-g-get that sack of flour for Libera. W-w-w-wait!

TITTA-NANE (*moving down front right: with exaggerated emulation*): Way-way-way-wait!

FORTUNATO (*following him ferociously*): What's the matter, what? What for you start squealing like a pig?

TITTA-NANE: Quiet! Here's your wife!

FORTUNATO: My wife! My wife! (FORTUNATO *turns apprehensively. He should be small and* LIBERA *big and buxom.*)

LIBERA (*entering left followed by* ORSETTA *and* CHECCA): What've you been doing? Why aren't you home yet?

FORTUNATO: I had to share out the fish. And how are you, wife? Have you been k-k-keeping well? And you, Orsetta? And Checca?

LIBERA: We are all well.

ORSETTA: And how is Titta-Nane? He seems very quiet.

TITTA-NANE (*gloomily down right*): Hello, there.

CHECCA: And not very friendly, either. Perhaps Lucietta's quarrelled with him.

TITTA-NANE: Yes, what's happened to Lucietta? She's not ill, is she?

ORSETTA: Ill! I'll say she isn't, the sweet thing!

TITTA-NANE: What's that supposed to mean? Have you and Lucietta been having trouble?

ORSETTA (*ironically*): Oh, how could you think such a thing?

CHECCA (*with irony*): Especially of Lucietta – who loves us all so much!

LIBERA: That'll be enough, you two. We all promised not to say anything about it. So don't let's give her any excuse for saying we're a lot of gossips.

FORTUNATO (*pushing in front of* TITTA-NANE – *annoyed at not receiving the attention of his wife and her sisters*): Well, wife, I've brought you what you w-w-w-wanted! A sack of flour! So now we'll be able to have some decent p-p-p-puddings!

LIBERA: Ay – well, I'll admit you're not a bad husband, when all's said and done.

FORTUNATO: And I've b-b-b-brought . . .

TITTA-NANE (*shoving* FORTUNATO *backwards out of the way and speaking to* LIBERA): Would you mind telling me just what . . .

FORTUNATO (*flying back at* TITTA *and pushing him away from* LIBERA): Will you k-keep quiet when your elders is speaking!

LIBERA (*soothingly, leading him down right*): Take it easy, luv! There's no need to speak like that.

TITTA-NANE (*following them*): Would you be so good as to tell me just what it is you all seem so angry with Lucietta about?

LIBERA (*maliciously*): Oh – just about nothing!

TITTA-NANE: Nothing?

ORSETTA (*nudging* LIBERA): Yes, that's all! About nothing. We're just angry with her about nothing!

CHECCA (*nudging* ORSETTA): Yes, a big, fat, lazy good-for-nothing NOTHING!

> FORTUNATO *watches with disgust their surreptitious nudges and giggles.*

FORTUNATO: Ach! W-w-w-women! (*Loudly*.) I'll g-go and fetch that sack of flour! (*Exit right*.)

TITTA-NANE: Well, you know, I wouldn't like to think that you and Lucietta weren't all good friends. I mean – I *know* you're all good girls. Just as I know Lucietta's a real pearl.

LIBERA (*with mock solemnity*): Oh, how right you are, Titta-Nane.

ORSETTA (*imitating* LIBERA): Oh, what a pearl!

CHECCA (*imitating them both*): Oh, indeed, yes – there aren't many pearls like *her*!

TITTA-NANE: Look – have you – or haven't you – got something against Lucietta?

ORSETTA: No, nothing!

CHECCA: Ask Monkey-face, if you don't believe us!

TITTA-NANE: Who's this – Monkey-face?

LIBERA: Quiet, both of you! What's got into you? Can't you hold your tongues?

TITTA-NANE (*getting excited*): Are you going to tell me who this Monkey-face is – or aren't you?

ORSETTA: You don't know Monkey-face Toffolo?

CHECCA: He's that ferryman. *You* know him.

> FORTUNATO *enters right, carrying a sack of flour over his shoulder.*

FORTUNATO (*to* TITTA-NANE): Come on, lad. T-t-t-time we all went home.

TITTA-NANE (*to* FORTUNATO, *sending him sprawling back*

C

right on top of his sack of flour): Oh, go to the devil! (*To the others.*) But what's he got to do with Lucietta?

CHECCA: Oh, he just sat down beside her, that's all.

ORSETTA: Yes, he was only wanting to learn how to make lace.

CHECCA (*ingenuously*): Oh, he was willing to pay – he gave her some sweetmeats!

LIBERA: And then the rascal – just to play up to her – started poking fun at us!

TITTA-NANE: By heavens, if this is true ...

> FORTUNATO *has pulled his sack of flour down front right, and, having got it over his shoulder once more, turns on* LIBERA.

FORTUNATO (*to* LIBERA): Let's all g-g-g-go home! Home! Home!

LIBERA (*to* TITTA-NANE): Started calling us all sorts of names!

CHECCA: He called me Sheep-face!

ORSETTA: And all because of your 'pearl'.

TITTA-NANE (*excitedly*): Where is he! Where can I find him? Where's he live? Where's he hiding himself?!

ORSETTA: He lives in the Calle della Corona, under the archway, where it comes out beside the canal.

LIBERA: Yes, he lives at home with his mother.

CHECCA: And he keeps his boat in the *rio del Palazzo*.

TITTA-NANE (*drawing his dagger and crossing down left*): Just you leave him to me! When I find him he'll wish the sharks had had him. I'll cut him up in little pieces!

CHECCA (*moving left centre after him*): Well, if you really want to find him, he's probably still with Lucietta.

TITTA-NANE: With Lucietta!

ORSETTA (*moving centre after them*): Yes – *you* know – your fiancée.

TITTA-NANE: Not any more, she isn't. I've done with her.
And as for that Monkey-face, I'll – I'll cut his liver out for
him when I find him! (*Exit left.*)

FORTUNATO(*to centre from down right*): That settles it! Home!
All of you! At once! Home! D-d-d'you hear me?

LIBERA: All right, all right, we're going – you old grumbler.

FORTUNATO: I'll have no more of your g-g-gossipping!
D'you hear? You start t-telling any more of your t-t-t-tales,
and I'll lock you all up in the house. D'you hear? I'll lock
you all up in the house! (*Exit left.*)

LIBERA (*turning to her sisters*): There! Now I hope you're
satisfied. My own husband turning on me, and all because
you can't hold your tongues. And after promising you
wouldn't say anything! (CHECCA *makes as if to interrupt.*)
Now, don't you start arguing with me! Go on, home with
you, both of you – before I really start losing my temper.
(*She shoos them off left, following them.*) Chatter, chatter,
chatter, that's all you can do! Go on, both of you, or I'll
box your ears for you, the pair of you!

Quick CURTAIN

Scene III

The same as Scene I. Later the same morning. TOFFOLO *enters
back-stage and comes down right looking about him apprehensively.*

TOFFOLO: I shouldn't have done it! I shouldn't have done
it! What on earth made me try to get off with Lucietta?
And she engaged to be married! I'm always being too
hasty! I should have kept on with Checca. She's still
young – but she certainly likes me. Or she wouldn't have

got so angry when I sat down by Lucietta. Yes, real jealous, she was! (*He turns and looks at the house, left.*) If I could only see her, I'd soon put matters right. I've a good mind to knock now. (*He goes to the door left.*) I wonder if she's in?

BEPPE *comes out of the door right.*

BEPPE: It's him, the rat!

TOFFOLO (*outside* FORTUNATO'S *door*): If she's not in, perhaps I'd better take care.

BEPPE: Hey – you – Mister Monkey-face!

TOFFOLO (*turning to him*): Are you speaking to me?

BEPPE: Yes, you! Get away from that door.

TOFFOLO: Why, what've I done to you?

BEPPE: You're standing too near that door.

TOFFOLO: But I'm just going to knock at it.

BEPPE: Oh, no, you're not.

TOFFOLO: Why shouldn't I?

BEPPE: Because I say so.

TOFFOLO: But what's it got to do with you?

BEPPE (*moving centre*): Are you going? Or have I got to make you?

TOFFOLO (*picking up a stone[1] in each hand from a small pile of them lying beside the house left*): Don't you come any nearer!

BEPPE (*pulling out his knife*): Right! You've asked for it!

TOFFOLO: But why should I go away? Why shouldn't I knock at this door?

BEPPE: Are you going?

TOFFOLO: Leave me alone! Why can't you leave me alone!

BEPPE: You'd better hurry, or I'll have your insides out!

TOFFOLO (*down left, raising his arm to throw a stone*): Get away – or I'll split your head open!

[1] see Introduction: Note to the Producer

BEPPE: Go on! Throw it!! (TONI *opens the door, right, behind him*.) Just let's see you throw it!

TONI: What's all this noise . . . (*He receives on his shoulder the stone* TOFFOLO *has thrown –* BEPPE *having dodged to one side*.)

TONI (*giving a loud yell*): So! You want to throw stones, eh? All right! You want a fight, eh? Well, just you wait there, then! Just you wait there! (*He dashes back into his house*.)

TOFFOLO (*calling after him*): *I* don't want to fight! It was he who started it!

BEPPE (*down right, his dagger raised*): Put down those stones.

TOFFOLO (*still down left*): You put that knife away!

TONI (*re-emerging holding a huge cutlass in his hand*): Now, we'll see who wants to throw stones!

PASQUA (*following* TONI *and seizing him by the arm*): Toni, stop it!

LUCIETTA (*also following and seizing him by the other arm*): Come back, brother.

BEPPE (*advancing on* TOFFOLO): Leave him to me, Captain Toni.

LUCIETTA (*leaving* TONI *and seizing* BEPPE *by the arm*): Don't be such a fool! Let him go!

TOFFOLO, *brave now that both men are being restrained, picks up some more stones.*

TOFFOLO (*preparing to throw another stone*): Get back inside, the lot of you – or I'll – I'll throw these stones at you! I will!

LUCIETTA (*shouting*): Help! Help!

PASQUA (*shouting*): Somebody come quickly! Murder! Help! Murder!

FORTUNATO, *followed by* LIBERA, ORSETTA *and* CHECCA, *dash out from their house.*

FORTUNATO: What is it? What's the matter? What's happening?

ORSETTA: It's a fight!

CHECCA: A fight? Oh, dear! (*She runs back into the house.*)

LIBERA: Stop this nonsense, all of you!

BEPPE: Nonsense? It was you lot who started it all!

ORSETTA: ⎱ Who!?
LIBERA: ⎰ Well, of all the nerve!

LUCIETTA (*releasing* BEPPE *and turning on* LIBERA *and* ORSETTA): Yes, it's all because you lot can't keep your silly tongues from wagging!

PASQUA: It's all you're any good at – making trouble!

ORSETTA: Oh! Did you ever hear such a wicked slander!

LIBERA: Why, they're nothing but a – but a couple of nasty-minded, back-biting she-devils!

The four women now start clawing and scratching each other. TONI *puts his cutlass on the bench and tries to grab hold of* PASQUA. FORTUNATO *tries to pull* LIBERA *away. Whilst this is going on in a group centre-stage,* TOFFOLO *and* BEPPE *are circling the group –* TOFFOLO *retreating, with a stone raised ready to throw, and* BEPPE *following, with his knife raised. When* TOFFOLO *has arrived down left,* BEPPE *suddenly yells.*

BEPPE (*down right, bellowing above the noise centre*): Will you get out of the way, all of you, and let me finish him off!

ORSETTA (*turning on him*): What are you *talking* about? Finish *who* off?

BEPPE (*shouting*): Who d'you think? That ape there! Monkey-face!

TOFFOLO (*throwing stones at them all*): Apes yourselves! Baboons! Yes! That's all you are! A lot of jabbering, gibbering, stuttering, hairy baboons!

The group centre scatters, PASQUA *now pulling* TONI, *and* LUCIETTA *pulling* BEPPE, *towards the door of their house.*

FORTUNATO, LIBERA *and* ORSETTA *all retreat to their side left,* TOFFOLO *goes centre stage, still with a stone at the ready and watching both sides warily.*

PASQUA (*pulling* TONI *by the arm*): Back – into the house – quickly!

LUCIETTA (*pulling* BEPPE *by the arm*): Please, brother, please, let's go in!

PASQUA (*as she pushes* TONI *through their door, right*): Do as I say! Inside! (*Exeunt* PASQUA *and* TONI.)

BEPPE (*to* LUCIETTA): Leave me alone!

LUCIETTA (*as she pushes* BEPPE *through their door, right*): Get in! Go on! Get inside! (*Exeunt* LUCIETTA *and* BEPPE, *closing their door after them.*)

TOFFOLO (*going over to their door, right*): Cowards! Assassins! Come out again, you lot of cowards!

ORSETTA (*shouting across to* TOFFOLO): Oh, go away and be quiet.

LIBERA: Yes, try jumping in a canal!

TOFFOLO (*turning*): So, you want to start something, too, do you?

FORTUNATO (*going up to him, excitedly*): Look, son, d-d-don't you start on me, or I'll just p-p-p-pull your g-guts out through your m-m-m-mouth, see?

TOFFOLO; Well, of course, I – er – respect *you* quite a lot, Fortunato, because you – er – well, you're Checca's brother-in-law – (*he turns towards* TONI'S *door*) – but, as for these rats, by heavens. I'll make them pay for this!

TITTA-NANE *enters right, behind* TOFFOLO, *carrying a large dagger in his hand.*

TITTA-NANE (*bellowing*): Ah!! So – *you* – are Monkey-face!!

TOFFOLO (*retreating towards door right*): Help! Help!

FORTUNATO (*to* TITTA-NANE): P-p-put that knife away and have some s-s-sense!

LIBERA (*holding* TITTA-NANE *by right arm*): Don't! You mustn't do it, Titta-Nane!

ORSETTA (*holding him by the left arm*): Hold him, Libera!

TITTA-NANE (*struggling towards* TOFFOLO): Let me go! Let me get at him!

TOFFOLO: Help! (*He presses himself against the door, right, which opens and he falls inside.*)

FORTUNATO (*also seizing* TITTA-NANE *and pulling him back*): Titta-Nane! Titta-Nane!

LIBERA (*to* FORTUNATO): Get him into our house! Get him into our house!

TITTA-NANE (*still struggling*): Leave me alone! I won't go!

FORTUNATO: It's for your own g-g-g-g-good, lad!
> *He twists his arm round* TITTA-NANE'S *neck and pulls him backwards, bodily, into their house, left, assisted by* LIBERA *and* ORSETTA. LIBERA *and* ORSETTA *are left alone on the stage, outside the door of their house.*

LIBERA: Oh! I'm trembling all over!

ORSETTA: My heart's beating like billy-o!
> TOFFOLO *suddenly erupts from the door right, chased by* PASQUA *and* LUCIETTA *and trying to shield his head with his arms from the rolling-pins which they are belabouring him with.*

PASQUA: Out you get! And don't you dare come into my house again! (*Goes in again.*)

LUCIETTA: Yes, did you ever see such a cheek! (*Goes in after* PASQUA *and closes the door.*)
> TOFFOLO *stands centre rubbing the back of his head.*

LIBERA: Serves you right! (*Goes into her house, left.*)

ORSETTA: It's a pity that head of yours is so thick! (*Follows* LIBERA, *left.*)

TOFFOLO (*alone – centre stage – shaking his fists at both houses*): By heavens, you've not heard the last of this! I'll have you all up, before the Court of Justice for this! D'you hear!

I'll make a complaint! I'll bring an action against you all!
All of you, d'you hear! Attempted murder, that's what it
was! I'll have you all sent to the galleys for this – d'you hear
me? All of you!

CURTAIN

ACT II

Scene I

Afternoon of the same day.
A room at the Chancellery. This scene played in front of tabs hiding
the permanent set. Small table right with flask of wine and glasses.
ISIDORO *is seated left at a table, writing with a quill pen. There is*
an empty chair centre facing his table. TOFFOLO *enters right,*
apprehensively.

TOFFOLO: Illustrious Signor Chancellor!
ISIDORO: I am not the Chancellor; I am the Commissioner,
   his assistant.
TOFFOLO: Illustrious Signor Commissioner!
ISIDORO: What is it you want?
TOFFOLO: I want to make a complaint, Illustrious! One of
   them tried to kill me with his knife, Illustrious, and then
   another of them came after me, Illustrious, and . . .
ISIDORO: There is no need to keep calling me Illustrious.
TOFFOLO: Yes, your Excellency. So long as you'll listen to
   me, Excellency. Oh, you should have heard the way they
   spoke to me, Excellency. And me not doing anything!
   They said to me – just as I'm speaking to you, Excellency –
   just like that – they said they wanted to kill me!
ISIDORO: Come, that's enough. Just wait a moment.
   He finds a pen and then looks for a piece of paper to write on.
TOFFOLO: Yes, of course, I'll wait, Illustrious! (*He walks*

down right, and mutters, aside.) Now to get my own back on them!

ISIDORO (*pointing to the chair, centre*): Sit down.

TOFFOLO *scurries across and sits eagerly on the edge of the chair.*

ISIDORO: Who are you?

TOFFOLO: I'm a ferryman, Illustrious.

ISIDORO: Your Christian name?

TOFFOLO: Toffolo.

ISIDORO: Surname?

TOFFOLO: Zavatta.

ISIDORO: Father alive?

TOFFOLO: My father died at sea, Illustrious.

ISIDORO: What was his name?

TOFFOLO: Toni Zavatta.

ISIDORO: And you, what's your nickname?

TOFFOLO: Me? *I* don't have one, Illustrious?

ISIDORO: Come, come! All you people give each other nicknames.

TOFFOLO: Well, couldn't you give me one, Illustrious?

ISIDORO: Don't be impertinent. Haven't I seen you here before?

TOFFOLO: Yes, Signor. I had to come here once for questioning.

ISIDORO: And your nickname then was – Monkey-face, I think.

TOFFOLO (*excitedly*): No, Illustrious! My name is Toffolo Zavatta, Illustrious.

ISIDORO: Take care I don't give you an 'Illustrious' on the head!

TOFFOLO: Have pity on me, your honour!

ISIDORO: Well, who *are* these people who've been threatening you?

TOFFOLO: Captain Toni Canestro, and his brother Beppe, and then Titta-Nane Moletto.

ISIDORO: Were they armed?

TOFFOLO: *I'll* say they were! Beppe had his fishing knife and Captain Toni had a huge cutlass that would have cut off the head of a bull and Titta-Nane had one of those daggers they use in fishing smacks!

ISIDORO: Did they wound you?

TOFFOLO: Well – no, but they certainly scared me, I can tell you.

ISIDORO: But why did they threaten you? Why did they attack you?

TOFFOLO: For no reason at all.

ISIDORO: Had there been any trouble? A quarrel? Had you been saying anything to them?

TOFFOLO: Me? I hadn't said a word to them!

ISIDORO: And you defended yourself? How did it all finish?

TOFFOLO: Well, there I was, like I said. So I said to them: Friends, I said, if you want to kill me, then kill me. That's what I said to them.

ISIDORO (*impatiently*): But – *how* did it all *end*?

TOFFOLO: Some good friends came along and made them stop – and saved my life.

ISIDORO: Who? Who were they – these good friends?

TOFFOLO: Fortunato Cavicchio and his wife Libera and her sister Orsetta and her other sister Checca.

ISIDORO (*as he writes*): So they're mixed up in it, are they? (*Aloud.*) Was anybody else present when the threats were made?

TOFFOLO: Captain Toni's wife, Donna Pasqua, and his sister, Lucietta.

ISIDORO (*aside, as he writes*): Those two – as well! So

that's how it is, is it? (*Aloud.*) Have you anything else to add?

TOFFOLO: No, that's all, Illustrious. Will you have them sent to the galleys, Illustrious?

ISIDORO: I'll have you sent to the gallows if you're not careful, you impertinent lout!

TOFFOLO: Me, your honour!

ISIDORO (*he rings the bell on his table*): That's enough. Since you've made this complaint, I suppose I shall have to look into it.

   POLICE-SERGEANT *enters.*

ISIDORO (*to* POLICE SERGEANT, *giving him list of names*): Arrange for these witnesses to be brought to me for questioning.

SERGEANT: Yes, sir.

TOFFOLO: Justice is all I want, Illustrious.

ISIDORO: Good day to you – Monkey-face. (*Exit.*)

TOFFOLO (*to the* SERGEANT, *laughing it off*): He likes to have his little joke, the Commissioner! He and I are great pals!

SERGEANT (*drily*): So I see. They're for you, are they – these witnesses?

TOFFOLO: Yes, sir! Yes, sergeant!

SERGEANT: You're quite sure you want them brought in for questioning?

TOFFOLO: Oh, yes, sergeant! All of them, sergeant!

SERGEANT: Ah! Well, it's thirsty work, you know, going around looking for people.

TOFFOLO: If you would do me the honour of having a drink with me?

SERGEANT: Well, if you insist, I'll not say no. Perhaps you'll be able to tell me, as well, where all these people live?

TOFFOLO (*as they go off together*): Oh, certainly, sergeant! As

a matter of fact, I *was* going to tell you that anyway. They
all live quite near each other down by the Zattere. . . .

CURTAIN

Scene II

The same as Act I, Scene I. Later the same afternoon. PASQUA *and*
LUCIETTA *come out of their house talking and carrying their lace-
frames. They sit and begin working without stopping talking.*

LUCIETTA: All the same, I do think it was mean of them to
go and tell Titta-Nane.

PASQUA: And what about you? Was there any need for you
to go and tell your brother about it all?

LUCIETTA: I suppose *you* didn't say anything yourself!

PASQUA: I'm not denying it. But I'm wishing now that I
hadn't.

LUCIETTA: Well, I'm sorry myself, if you really want to
know. I swear I'll never open my mouth to those women
again. Never!

PASQUA: It was always the same. Believe me, if we women
couldn't gossip a little now and then, we'd burst. But
what's upsetting me is that our menfolk have been dragged
into their silly squabble.

LUCIETTA: I wouldn't worry over that. That Toffolo's
nothing but a silly booby. He won't do anything about
it.

PASQUA: Beppe is ready to break with Orsetta.

LUCIETTA: Oh, well – he'll soon find somebody else, if he
does. There are plenty of good girls in Venice.

PASQUA (*drily*): That's just the point. Out of forty thousand people, thirty thousand of them are women!

LUCIETTA: And so most of them aren't married – is that what you mean?

PASQUA: Exactly! If Titta-Nane should break off his engagement with *you*, you wouldn't find it so easy to find another young man.

LUCIETTA: But what've *I* done to Titta-Nane?

PASQUA: Don't upset yourself. *You* haven't done anything. It's those gossips, over there, who've made him angry with you.

LUCIETTA: But *why* can't he trust me? *Why* does he even listen to their tittle-tattling?

PASQUA: Don't you see – he's jealous.

LUCIETTA: What reason's he got to be jealous, I'd like to know? Can't one open one's mouth now? The men are away at sea for months on end, while we've got to sit here growing mouldy and rotten with nothing to do but chew the cud over these confounded lace-frames!

PASQUA: Quiet! Here's Titta-Nane now!

TITTA-NANE *has appeared back-stage, but when he sees them he hesitates, then turns and remains back-stage, pretending to be looking along the canal, off stage.*

LUCIETTA: Yes, just look at him! I can tell at a glance he's going to sulk. The big baby!

PASQUA: Now don't start an argument. Just let him talk his head off.

LUCIETTA: He never stops doing that. Why shouldn't *I*, for a change?

PASQUA: Look, are you really in love with him?

LUCIETTA: Oh, you know I am!

PASQUA: Well, give in. Apologize to him. Say you're sorry.

TITTA-NANE *walks down front left.*

LUCIETTA: Me? Not likely!

PASQUA: Don't be so stubborn!

LUCIETTA: I'd rather jump in the canal!

PASQUA: Oh, you're impossible! I've no patience left with you!

TITTA-NANE (*aside, down left*): I've finished with her – but I don't know how to tell her.

PASQUA (*to* LUCIETTA): Just give him a smile. Go on, just look at him!

LUCIETTA (*to* PASQUA): I've got my lace to look at. I must keep my eyes on my lace-frame!

PASQUA (*aside*): I'd like to bang your head with your lace-frame!

TITTA-NANE (*aside*): She doesn't look at me. She doesn't even look at me.

PASQUA: Good-morning, Titta-Nane.

TITTA-NANE: Good-morning.

PASQUA (*aside to* LUCIETTA): Say good-morning.

LUCIETTA: Not likely. It's up to him to speak first.

TITTA-NANE (*moving centre, after a pause*): You both seem very busy this morning.

PASQUA: And why not? We've a lot to do.

TITTA-NANE (*sarcastically*): Yes, of course. It's best to get it done while you can, isn't it? There won't be much time for work when the young fellows come snooping around, will there?

LUCIETTA (*sardonically*): Hah! Hah!

PASQUA (*aside to* LUCIETTA): Speak to him!

LUCIETTA (*aside to* PASQUA): Never!

TITTA-NANE (*to* PASQUA): Donna Pasqua, do you like roasted sweetmeats?

PASQUA: Now why ask me that?

TITTA-NANE: Oh – just that I fancy one myself at the moment.

LUCIETTA (*without taking her eyes from her work*): Roasted sweetmeats make me spit.

TITTA-NANE (*aside, moving back front left*): Oh, I could – strangle her!

A pause. The women go on working.

TITTA-NANE (*aside*): Well, she's asked for it! (*He returns centre and speaks to* PASQUA.) Donna Pasqua – I address myself to you for *you're* a lady – I wish to inform you that I am now breaking off my engagement to your sister-in-law, Lucietta.

PASQUA: But what on earth for? What on earth d'you want to do that for?

TITTA-NANE (*looking at* LUCIETTA): Because . . . because . . .

LUCIETTA *rises.*

PASQUA (*to* LUCIETTA): Where are you going?

LUCIETTA: Where I please. (*She dashes into her house, right.*)

PASQUA (*to* TITTA-NANE): Why do you have to go on believing a lot of tittle-tattle – a lot of women's gossip?

TITTA-NANE: I know *all* about it – and I must say I'm surprised at *you* – I'm surprised at *her* . . .

PASQUA (*rises and goes up to him, centre*): Let *me* tell *you* something, young man. That girl loves you very much indeed.

TITTA-NANE: Then she's got a funny way of showing it. What's she want to get up for now and go in like that for?

PASQUA: Poor child! She's gone in to weep; yes, that's what she's gone in for – to have a good cry?

TITTA-NANE: Who for? Monkey-face?

PASQUA (*seriously and with dignity*): No, Titta-Nane. It's you she loves. Whenever you go to sea, she's so miserable she doesn't know what to do with herself. And when you're

away, and the sea is rough, she nigh goes out of her mind
worrying over you. She even gets up in the middle of the
night, just to see what the weather's like. You understand,
I'm telling you this because I have seen it with my own eyes.

TITTA-NANE: But why doesn't she give me one kind word?
Just one? Why?

PASQUA: Because you frighten her.

TITTA-NANE: Aren't I in the right at all, then?

PASQUA: Look, I will tell you how it all happened.

TITTA-NANE: No, Donna Pasqua, I want *her* to tell me that
herself. And I want her to ask me to forgive her.

PASQUA: And will you forgive her?

TITTA-NANE: Who knows? Maybe I will . . . anyway,
where is she? Where has she got to?

PASQUA: Here she is! Here she is now!

LUCIETTA *comes out of the house.*

LUCIETTA (*to* TITTA-NANE): Here, sir, are the ribbons, the
slippers and the keepsakes which you gave me! (*She throws
them on to the ground in front of him.*)

PASQUA: Have you gone daft, girl! (*She picks them up and puts
them on the bench.*)

TITTA-NANE (*slowly and sorrowfully*): What did you want to
do *that* for?

LUCIETTA (*sitting on right end of their bench*): Haven't you just
broken off our engagement? Take your presents and – and
– do what you like with them!

TITTA-NANE (*striding centre, explosively*): If – if you speak
another *word* to Monkey-face, I'll – I'll kill him!

LUCIETTA: What concern is it of yours now who I speak to?

TITTA-NANE: It's because of him I've broken our engagement. *That's* why!

PASQUA: How *could* you think Lucietta would ever have
anything to do with that sort of a fellow?

TITTA-NANE: Then why has he been hanging round here? And why did she let him buy her roasted sweetmeats?

LUCIETTA: Is that a crime?

PASQUA: Oh, what a to-do about nothing!

TITTA-NANE: What! Is it *nothing* that I shouldn't wish people to be able to gossip about the girl I'm going to marry? (*Moving back, down front left.*) By heavens, I'll see nobody pokes fun at me behind my back! Nobody!

LUCIETTA (*wiping her eyes*): What a thin skin you must have!

TITTA-NANE (*facing audience*): I'm a *man*, that's what I am! Not a monkey-faced bit of a boy!

   LUCIETTA *is weeping but making an effort not to show it.*

PASQUA (*to* LUCIETTA): What's the matter?

LUCIETTA (*still weeping, she nudges* PASQUA *and makes gestures not to take any notice*): Nothing!

PASQUA (*aside*): You're crying!

LUCIETTA (*aside*): Yes, with rage! I could strangle him with my own hands!

TITTA-NANE (*going up to* LUCIETTA *with rough concern*): Now then! Now then! What's all the tears for, eh?

LUCIETTA (*miserably*): Oh, *go* to the devil!

TITTA-NANE (*to* PASQUA): There you are! You heard her! Go to the devil, she said!

PASQUA: And so you'd better, if you're going to go on behaving like this!

TITTA-NANE (*after gazing at them both, in bafflement*): I suppose you think *I'd* never chuck *myself* into a canal.

PASQUA: Oh, stop talking nonsense.

LUCIETTA (*still weeping*): Oh, make him go away! Make him go away!

PASQUA (*turning to* LUCIETTA): And you – if you ask me you're nearly as daft as he is!

TITTA-NANE (*sorrowfully, moving down left*): And I loved her. I loved her dearly.

PASQUA (*to* TITTA-NANE): And you don't any more, eh?

TITTA-NANE: How can I? If she doesn't want me?

PASQUA (*to* LUCIETTA): What do *you* say to that?

LUCIETTA: Oh, leave me alone, let me alone!

PASQUA (*to* LUCIETTA): Take back your slippers and your ribbons and your trinkets.

LUCIETTA: I don't want them – I don't want anything.

PASQUA: Listen to me.

LUCIETTA: Let me alone!

PASQUA: Just say one word to him.

LUCIETTA: No!

PASQUA (*to* TITTA-NANE): You come over here.

TITTA-NANE: Never!

PASQUA: Then go away and stop troubling us.

TITTA-NANE: I don't want to go away.

PASQUA (*disgustedly, going on with her lace-making*): Oh! Then for heaven's sake, will you stop behaving like a couple of silly children! Both of you!

    The SERGEANT *enters backstage and comes briskly down to* PASQUA.

SERGEANT (*to* PASQUA): Are you Donna Pasqua, wife of Captain Toni Canestro?

PASQUA (*rising again*): Yes, sir. Can I be of service to you, sir?

SERGEANT: And this is Lucietta, sister of Captain Toni?

PASQUA: Yes, sir. But what do you want with her?

SERGEANT: I have an order here summoning you both (LUCIETTA *rises*) to appear immediately for questioning at the Chancellery.

PASQUA: For questioning? But what for?

SERGEANT: I know nothing about it – except that you will be fined ten ducats if you do not obey the summons.

PASQUA (*drawing* LUCIETTA *down front right and speaking aside*): It must be about that row yesterday!

LUCIETTA (*aside to* PASQUA): I don't want to go.

PASQUA (*aside to* LUCIETTA): But we'll have to!

SERGEANT (*to* PASQUA, *after examining the house opposite*): Is that the house of Fortunato?

PASQUA: Yes, indeed, sir, it is!

SERGEANT: Well, that's all I want with you. As the door seems to be open, I'll walk in. (*Goes into* FORTUNATO'S *house.*)

PASQUA: Did you hear that, Titta-Nane?

TITTA-NANE: I heard. That scoundrel Monkey-face must be going to take me to court over it all. I'll just have to disappear for a while, that's all!

PASQUA: And what about my husband?

LUCIETTA: And my brothers?

PASQUA: Oh, this is terrible! (*To* LUCIETTA.) Go! Go quickly to the harbour and if you find them, warn them at once. I'll go and find Vincenzo. I'll go and see the Chancellor himself! Oh, what have we done for this to happen to us!

Goes left quickly.

TITTA-NANE: Now you see what you've done!

LUCIETTA: What I've done! I like that! Why me?

TITTA-NANE: Of all the brainless idiots!

LUCIETTA (*moving front right*): Oh, go away, you big ape!

TITTA-NANE (*following her*): Yes, you'll be quite happy if they send me away, won't you?

LUCIETTA: Who? Why should *who* send you away?

TITTA-NANE (*going front centre*): If *they* banish me from Venice – I'll kill that Monkey-face first!

LUCIETTA (*following him*): Have you gone quite mad!?

TITTA-NANE: And you! I'll make you pay for it, as well!

SERGEANT *and* FORTUNATO *come out of house left and stand by the door making mock conversation.*

LUCIETTA: Look out! Here's that Sergeant again.

TITTA-NANE (*as he goes, right*): All right! I'll go before he sees me! Not that *he'd* be able to stop me, though! And don't you forget what I've just been saying! (*Exit right.*)

LUCIETTA (*front right*): Oh, the beast! Starting to threaten *me* now! Oh, men! Men! If any of them ever speak to me about marriage again, I'll – I'll throw myself in the canal! (*Exit right.*)

The SERGEANT *and* FORTUNATO *come front centre.*

SERGEANT: Well, that's how it is, Fortunato. But you're a man of the world and so you know how these things are. It's just a matter of form. A bit of red tape.

FORTUNATO (*excited: stuttering violently*): Me! G-g-go down there! Understand? No? N-never b-b-been down there! Chancellery! N-never b-been to Chancellery!

SERGEANT: You've never been to the Chancellery!

FORTUNATO: No, sir! Never, sir! N-n-never!

SERGEANT: Well, well! You don't say so!

FORTUNATO: And my wife! W-w-why m-must she go – as well?

SERGEANT: To be questioned.

FORTUNATO: And b-b-both her sisters as well?

SERGEANT: Both of them.

FORTUNATO: Even the young one? The little one?

SERGEANT: She'll be with your wife. What are you frightened of?

FORTUNATO: She's c-c-crying! Frightened, she is! She d-d-doesn't want to go!

SERGEANT: Well, if she doesn't come, it will be the worse for her! I'm just carrying out my orders, that's all. The rest is up to you. I'd think it over, if I were you! (*Exit right.*)

FORTUNATO (*excitedly*): We're going to have to go! We'll
have to! We'll all have to go! (*Shouts towards his door.*) Wife!
– Get your shawl on, wife! Orsetta! Put your shawl on too!
Checca, put yours on as well, because you'll have to go!
(*Coming front and speaking to the audience.*) We'll have to g-go!
We'll have to! The d-devil take all w-women! G-gossip-
ping – tittle-tattling lot of trouble-makers! (*Shouts again
towards his door.*) Hurry up in there! What are youse all
d-doing now? Women! Women! Nothing but trouble!
(*Bellows.*) Are youse all coming – or do I give youse a taste
of my stick? Yes, a taste of my stick – that's what I give
youse! (*Goes into his house with raised stick.*) A taste of my
stick!

CURTAIN

Scene III

As Act II, Scene I: The Chancellery; later the same afternoon.
VINCENZO *is standing before* ISIDORO, *who is seated at his table.*

VINCENZO: But if your Excellency would just consider.
The whole business is really all nothing but a storm in a
teacup.
ISIDORO: I have not said that it isn't. But a complaint has
been made, the witnesses have been summoned, the case
has been opened. So Justice will have to take its course.
VINCENZO: Look, Illustrious, d'yer really believe that that
chap – you know who – the feller that's making the
complaint – is as innocent as 'e looks? Well, let me tell you
something – 'e went a sight further than they did – 'e was
throwing stones at them!

ISIDORO: All the better. The inquiry will reveal the truth.

VINCENZO: Couldn't perhaps some arrangement be come to, Illustrious?

ISIDORO: It is true that an arrangement could be arrived at, out of court – *if* the plaintiff were agreeable, and if all costs were paid.

VINCENZO: Look, Illustrious, you know me. I'm a blunt man. Put yer cards on the table – and let's both stop beating about the bush!

ISIDORO: All right, I'll be frank with you, Vincenzo. The matter *could* be arranged out of court – the plaintiff's deposition contains hardly anything except a lot of trifles. But we do not know yet what the witnesses will say. I must at least question some of them. If, however, nothing else then comes to light, if this brawl was not premeditated, if there has been no abuse of authority, no injury to third parties, or things of that nature, I will be the first to agree to an accommodation. All the same the final decision even then would not rest with me. I am the Commissioner and not the Chancellor. I have to make a report to my superior. The Chancellor is in Padua, but we are expecting his return at any moment. He will then take a quick look into this little matter. *You* can have a word with him; *I* will have a word with him. What do I get out of it, after all? And you know I am not just being officious – I'm an easy-going man and don't go out of my way to make work for myself. On the other hand, I like to intercede for people and do what I can to help them.

VINCENZO: Thank you, Illustrious. If I might say so, that was spoken like the honest man that you are. I see now what has to be done.

ISIDORO: As for me, as I've said, I want nothing at all!

VINCENZO: Not even some fish? Some fine fish?

ISIDORO: Some fine fish, eh? We don't eat badly at the Chancellery, but a nice little tit-bit, now and then, is always welcome.

VINCENZO: I've always said yer Excellency was a good judge of them sort of things.

ISIDORO: You know how it is. One works, one slaves away, one must have a little enjoyment, now and then, of the finer things of life! But it's time I got ready for – the interrogation. (*Rises.*) No, no, you stay here, my old friend, and if these people arrive, tell them I shall be back in a moment. And tell the women that they've only come for questioning, they need have no fear. I like to be on friendly terms with everyone, but especially with the ladies, bless 'em! (*Exit left.*)

VINCENZO (*alone*): Yes, Mister Commissioner, you're a fine gentleman – but that don't count much with me. (*He looks off stage, right, rises, and comes left centre.*) Ah, this sounds like them, now.

PASQUA, LUCIETTA, LIBERA, ORSETTA, CHECCA, *all with shawls over their heads, and* FORTUNATO, *enter right.*

VINCENZO (*front left*): Come in, everyone! Come on in, that's right! Make yerselves at home. We're all old friends here!

CHECCA (*looking round fearfully*): Where are we?

ORSETTA (*also not her usual pert self*): Where are we going?

LIBERA: Oh, dear me! I never thought I'd ever find myself in this place!

FORTUNATO (*shaking* VINCENZO *by the hand*): 'Incenzo! Here's old 'Incenzo! Fancy m-meeting old 'Incenzo here of all p-p-places!

VINCENZO: Fortunato! Good to see yer again, old chap!

FORTUNATO (*to* VINCENZO): The   Ch-ch-chancellor! Where is he?

VINCENZO: Oh, *he* isn't here. He's in Padua. It's the Commissioner who's going to see you.

LIBERA (*to* ORSETTA, *nudging her to indicate that it's the Commissioner they all know so well*): Did you hear? It's the old fellow, the Commissioner!

ORSETTA (*to* CHECCA, *nudging her and laughing*): Fancy, it's that nice old Commissioner!

PASQUA (*happy again, to* LUCIETTA): That's all right! It's only the Commissioner who's going to question us.

LUCIETTA (*to* PASQUA): I suppose it could be worse. At least we know him well enough!

PASQUA (*to* LUCIETTA): Oh, he's a real gentleman, the Commissioner is!

ISIDORO enters left.

ISIDORO (*coming irately centre*): What are you all doing in here?

ALL THE WOMEN: Illustrious! Excellency! Illustrious!

ISIDORO: But this won't do! No! No! This won't do! D'you think I can question you all at the same time! Go outside and wait and I will call you in one at a time.

PASQUA: Us first!

LUCIETTA: We were first!

ORSETTA: No, you don't! It's us who were first!

ISIDORO: I will be quite fair to everyone. I'll call you, in the order you are on this paper. Checca is the first. Let Checca stay here and the rest of you go outside and wait.

PASQUA: Fair enough! She's the youngest, after all.

LUCIETTA: And the luckiest, evidently.

FORTUNATO: Outside! Outside! All of youse! Out, with yer! (LUCIETTA, PASQUA *and* LIBERA *go off right*.)

ORSETTA (*coyly*): Oh, Illustrious! You won't keep her too long, will you? We have to get back to our work, you know!

ISIDORO: Never fear. I shall be as quick as possible.

> FORTUNATO *pushes* ORSETTA *out through the door right. They are followed by* VINCENZO. ISIDORO *goes to his table and sits behind it.*

ISIDORO (*to* CHECCA, *who is still standing near the door*): Come over here, and sit down.

CHECCA: I'd rather stand, your Excellency.

ISIDORO (*loudly*): Sit down. (*More quietly as she comes and sits in the chair facing him.*) I do not like to see ladies standing while I am seated.

CHECCA: Whatever you wish, sir.

ISIDORO: What is your name?

CHECCA: My name is Checca.

ISIDORO: Yes, I know that. What is your *surname*?

CHECCA: Schiantina.

ISIDORO: And you have a nickname?

CHECCA: Certainly not! What an idea! A nickname, indeed?

ISIDORO: You are not called – Sheep-face, then?

CHECCA: Are you going to make fun of me, as well?

ISIDORO: Never mind. I see you are a good girl. Now, tell me. Do you know why I sent for you to come here?

CHECCA: Yes, sir, because of the quarrel.

ISIDORO: Tell me how it all happened. (ISIDORO *writes as she speaks.*)

CHECCA: But I don't know anything about it. I wasn't there. I went back into our house with my sister Libera, and with my sister Orsetta, and with my brother-in-law Fortunato. There was Captain Toni, and Beppe, and Titta-Nane who wanted to give Monkey-face Toffolo a good hiding, and *he* was throwing stones at them.

ISIDORO: Why did Titta-Nane want to give – er – Monkey-face a good hiding?

CHECCA: Because Titta-Nane is courting Lucietta and

because Monkey-face had just been speaking to her *and* buying her sweetmeats.

ISIDORO: I understand. That will do. (*A short pause while he writes.*) How old are you?

CHECCA: How old am I?

ISIDORO: That's what I said. Everybody who is questioned here has to give their age, and it is put at the end of their statement. So, what is your age?

CHECCA: Oh, *I've* no need to hide it. I'm just seventeen.

ISIDORO: You swear that you have told the truth?

CHECCA: What about?

ISIDORO: Do you swear that what you have said in the course of this interrogation has been the truth?

CHECCA: Oh, yes, I swear it's all the truth.

ISIDORO: Your interrogation is finished.

CHECCA: May I go then?

ISIDORO: One moment, please. All those young men of yours. How are they all?

CHECCA: My young men? But I haven't even *got one*!

ISIDORO: You must not tell lies to me.

CHECCA: Will I have to swear to it?

ISIDORO: No, you are no longer on oath. All the same, it is wicked to tell lies. So, let us see then, how many young men is it that you have?

CHECCA: Nobody wants me. Because I am poor.

ISIDORO: What if I arranged for you to have a dowry?

CHECCA: Oh, Excellency!

ISIDORO: If you had a dowry, you *would* get married?

CHECCA: Of course I would, oh, of course I would, Illustrious!

ISIDORO: Is there no young man who's taken your fancy? (*She is silent.*) Well, what about one who makes you lose your temper?

CHECCA (*coyly*): You are making me blush. . . .

ISIDORO: What on earth is there to blush about? We are alone. You can speak quite freely in here.

CHECCA: Well, if I could have him, Titta-Nane would suit me fine.

ISIDORO: But I thought he was in love with Lucietta?

CHECCA: He's broken it off with her.

ISIDORO: If that is so, we might see what could be done. . . .

CHECCA: How much would the dowry be?

ISIDORO: About fifty ducats.

CHECCA: Oh, sir! And my brother-in-law would give me a *hundred*, and I've got another *fifty* saved from my lace-making! I don't believe even Lucietta would have as much!

ISIDORO: Do you wish me to speak to Titta-Nane?

CHECCA: Oh, yes, please, Excellency!

ISIDORO: Where is he, by the way?

CHECCA: He's – hiding.

ISIDORO: Ah! And where is he hiding?

CHECCA: Well – I'll whisper it to you. I wouldn't like any-one to hear me. (*She rises and whispers in his ear.*)

ISIDORO: I understand. I will have him brought here. I'll question him myself – leave it to me. All right, run along, child. Off with you, now, and mind you – not a word of this to anyone. Understand? (*He rings his bell.*)

CHECCA: May Heaven bless you, Excellency!

SERGEANT (*entering*): Excellency!

ISIDORO: Bring Orsetta in.

SERGEANT: Yes, sir. (*Exit.*)

ISIDORO (*to* CHECCA): I will keep you informed. I will come and see you.

CHECCA: Yes, Excellency. (*She rises.*) Oh, if I only could take him from Lucietta! If only I could!

    ORSETTA *enters right.*

ORSETTA (*aside to* CHECCA): You've been a long time! What's he been asking you?

CHECCA (*to* ORSETTA): Oh, sister, the things he's been asking! I'll tell you all about it! (*Exit right.*)

ISIDORO: Come over here and sit down!

ORSETTA: Certainly, sir. (*She sits with cool self-assurance.*)

ISIDORO (*aside*): An impudent hussy, this one! (*Aloud.*) How are you called?

ORSETTA: Orsetta Schiantina.

ISIDORO: I mean – what else are you called?

ORSETTA: What else?

ISIDORO: You have a nickname, haven't you?

ORSETTA: If you say so.

ISIDORO: Don't they call you Pasty-face?

ORSETTA: If we were anywhere else but in your stupid Chancellery, I'd knock your silly wig off for that!

ISIDORO: Now, now, there's no need to be disrespectful!

ORSETTA: Well, what's the idea? Bringing me here just to insult me!

ISIDORO: It has to be entered on the deposition as a relevant fact. So calm yourself. Besides, you know very well why you are here.

ORSETTA: No, sir.

ISIDORO: You can't even give a guess?

ORSETTA: No, sir.

ISIDORO: You mean to say you haven't heard anything at all about a certain quarrel?

ORSETTA: I might have and then again I mightn't.

ISIDORO: That's enough! Just tell me what you know about it!

ORSETTA: You ask the questions and I'll give the answers.

ISIDORO: Do you know Toffolo Zavatta?

ORSETTA: No, sir.

ISIDORO: Monkey-face Toffolo?

ORSETTA: Oh yes, I know him!

ISIDORO: And you also know, do you not, that certain people wanted to give him a good hiding?

ORSETTA: How should I know what people *want* to do?

ISIDORO: Have you seen anybody threatening him – with any kind of weapon?

ORSETTA: Yes, sir.

ISIDORO: Who?

ORSETTA: I don't quite remember who.

ISIDORO: If I give you some names, will that help you to remember?

ORSETTA: Oh, yes, if you name them, I'll be able to remember them!

ISIDORO (*rises exasperated and comes front left muttering, aside*): This little devil's trying to keep me here all day! (*Aloud.*) Titta-Nane – was he one of them?

ORSETTA: Yes, sir!

ISIDORO: Captain Toni – was he there?

ORSETTA: Yes, sir!

ISIDORO: Beppe, Captain Toni's brother, was he there?

ORSETTA: Yes, sir!

ISIDORO (*sitting at his table again*): Well done, Pasty-face!

ORSETTA: Tell me, has nobody ever given you a nickname?

ISIDORO (*writing*): Now then, that'll do! Less of the impudence, please.

ORSETTA: Because I'll give you one if you like. What about 'Old Skinflint'?

ISIDORO: Did Monkey-face Toffolo throw some stones?

ORSETTA: Yes, he did throw some. (*Aside.*) A pity he doesn't throw some at you.

ISIDORO: What was that?

ORSETTA: Nothing. Can't one speak to oneself now?

ISIDORO: Well, what was it that started the quarrel?

ORSETTA: How should I know?

ISIDORO (*aside*): Maybe she's trying to drive me mad! (*Aloud, with exaggerated patience.*) Did you know that Titta-Nane was jealous of Monkey-face?

ORSETTA: Of course! Everybody knows that! Because of Lucietta.

ISIDORO: And did you know that Titta-Nane had broken off his engagement to Lucietta?

ORSETTA: Oh, yes, everybody knows that as well!

ISIDORO (*aside*): So Checca was telling the truth. (*Aloud.*) Well, that seems to be all. How old are you?

ORSETTA: Dearie me, he's even got to know my age as well!

ISIDORO: Yes, Miss, your age as well.

ORSETTA: And you're going to write it down there?

ISIDORO: Yes, I have to write it down here.

ORSETTA: All right, then put down that I'm nineteen.

ISIDORO (*writing*): Swear that you have told the truth!

ORSETTA: Swear what?

ISIDORO: That you have spoken the truth.

ORSETTA: Oh, well, put down twenty-four.

ISIDORO: It's not a question of swearing on oath as to your age! How on earth can one ask any woman to do that! All I'm asking you to do is to swear that you have given true answers to all those other questions I've been asking you!

ORSETTA: Oh, yes, I'll swear to those all right.

> ISIDORO *rings the bell beside him and the* SERGEANT *enters right.*

SERGEANT: Who next, Excellency?

ISIDORO: Donna Libera.

SERGEANT: Yes, sir. (*Exit.*)

ORSETTA (*aside, as she rises and crosses to the door*): Well, I don't know! Fancy wanting to know your age, now!

LIBERA enters as ORSETTA reaches the door. ISIDORO goes on writing at his table.

LIBERA (*aside to ORSETTA*): How did you get on?

ORSETTA (*aside*): Just imagine! He even wants to know how old you are!

LIBERA (*aside*): No! You're joking!

ORSETTA (*aside to LIBERA*): *And* you have to swear to it! (*Exit right.*)

LIBERA (*aside, coming front right*): What? Give your age and then have to swear to it! We'll see about that! I'm not likely to go telling him my age, and I've certainly no intention whatever of swearing to it!

ISIDORO: All right, come over here and sit down.

LIBERA remains standing where she is and makes no reply.

ISIDORO (*loudly*): Come here and sit down!

He points to the chair in front of him and LIBERA crosses and sits in it.

ISIDORO: What is your name?

LIBERA does not reply.

ISIDORO (*loudly*): Answer me! What is your name?

LIBERA: Sir?

ISIDORO (*shouting*): What's your name?

LIBERA: What did you say?

ISIDORO (*bellowing*): Are you deaf?

LIBERA: I'm a little hard of hearing, sir.

ISIDORO (*aside*): I must keep calm! (*Aloud, with forced control.*) How do you call yourself?

LIBERA: I beg your pardon?

ISIDORO (*loudly, thumping the table with his fist*): Your name!?

LIBERA: A little louder – if you wouldn't mind.

E

ISIDORO (*rising and ringing his bell violently*): No! No! I will not be driven mad!

SERGEANT (*entering*): Excellency?

ISIDORO: Bring the man in.

SERGEANT: At once, sir.

ISIDORO (*to* LIBERA): And you – you go and wash your ears out!

LIBERA: Sir?

ISIDORO (*pushing her towards the door right*): Out! Get out of here! I've had enough! I can't stand much more! (*Exit* LIBERA.)

He walks back to his table holding his hands to his head.

ISIDORO: I must try to remember I am the Commissioner. It's a fine position to have, an honest one, a worth-while one – even a useful one! But I think that sometimes it could drive me mad!

FORTUNATO *erupts into the room from the right and manages to bring himself to a halt in front of the table. In his nervousness, his arms and head are twitching violently. He collapses exhausted into the chair.*

FORTUNATO: 'Lustrious! x-x-x-xc'Hency!

ISIDORO: What is your name?

FORTUNATO: Fort-t-t-t-tunato 'Vichio.

ISIDORO: Speak clearly if you want to make yourself understood. I'll assume you were saying that you are Fortunato Cavicchio. Do you know the reason why you are here?

FORTUNATO: Oh, yes, sir!

ISIDORO: *Good!* Why are you here, then?

FORTUNATO: B-b-b-because the sergeant t-told me to c-c-come!

ISIDORO (*aside*): Another of them! (*Aloud.*) I *know* you're here because the Sergeant told you to come! Tell me – *do* you know anything about a certain quarrel?

FORTUNATO: Oh, yes, sir!

ISIDORO: Well, tell me. How did it all start?

FORTUNATO: Yes, sir! Well, sir! I c-came back s'morning –
in the fishing smack – and my wife c-came down to the
harbour and my sister-in-law Orsetta and my sister-in-law
Checca – they all c-c-came t-t-too.

ISIDORO: I have just told you that if you don't speak clearly,
I won't be able to understand you.

FORTUNATO: Yes, sir! Yes, sir! Well, sir, g-g-going b-back
home, I saw C-c-captain Toni and his b-b-brother B-B-
Beppe. And Titta-Nane and Monkey-face! (*He jumps to his
feet and makes a wide slashing movement with arms.*) And
C-C-Captain Toni – swish – b-big sword! (*Another slashing
movement so violent he almost falls over.*) And B-B-Beppe –
wheeee – knife! (*He jumps in the air, banging loudly on the floor
with his feet.*) And Monkey-face – bang, bang – with stones!
(*He hurls himself up on to the chair and stands there, his arms
flaying the air.*) Then Titta-Nane c-comes – slash – dagger!
Everybody – all over place! (*He collapses exhausted and sits
sprawling in the chair. Then manages to say*) That just all I
know. Clear? You understand me, eh?

ISIDORO (*in a whisper*): Not a word! (*Loudly.*) Not one single
damn' word!

FORTUNATO: But I speak our language! What country you
come from, 'Llustrious?

ISIDORO: I come from Venice, you fool! And I've not
understood one word you've said!

FORTUNATO: You order me to 'peat?

ISIDORO: What?

FORTUNATO (*shouting*): You order me – '*peat* all I say?

ISIDORO (*standing, holding his hands to his head*): Get out! Get
out! Get out!

FORTUNATO (*retreating*): 'Ut 'issimo!

ISIDORO (*advancing after him*): Damn' – parrot!

FORTUNATO (*retreating further*): 'Ut 'issimo!

ISIDORO: Heaven help me if I ever have you lot on my hands in a real law suit!

FORTUNATO (*opening the door right*): 'Ut 'issimo! (*Exit.*)

ISIDORO (*going back to his table*): And may the devil take the lot of you! (*He rings his bell*).

SERGEANT (*entering*): Excellency?

ISIDORO: Send those other two women away! At once! I don't want to hear any more – from any of them!

SERGEANT: Yes, sir! (*Exit.*)

ISIDORO (*goes to table right and pours himself a glass of wine*): All the same, I really must remember my position. Yes, in future, I shall have to try to exercise a little more patience. Yes, that's it. I simply must not allow myself to lose patience like this.

He has just re-seated himself at his table, left, when PASQUA *and* LUCIETTA *erupt into the room, right.*

PASQUA (*violently*): Why are you sending us away?

LUCIETTA: Why don't you want to question us?

ISIDORO: Enough! Enough! No more!

PASQUA: Oh, *we* understand! *We* know *your* little game!

LUCIETTA: Yes, he listens to those he wants to keep in with, but we others – oh, we can be shown the way out, we can!

ISIDORO: Have you finished?

PASQUA: Old Pasty-face – he kept her in here nearly an hour!

LUCIETTA: And Sheep-face, how long was she in here?

PASQUA: Well, we'll go where we will be listened to!

LUCIETTA: And where we'll get some justice, as well!

ISIDORO: Listen to me, you ignorant pair! You just don't know what you're talking about!

PASQUA: Oh, don't we?

LUCIETTA: Thinks he knows better, I suppose!

ISIDORO: You two belong to the opposite party. You're the defendants. So you can't serve as witnesses!

LUCIETTA: *That*'s not true! That's *not* true! We're not the defendants! That's not true at all!

PASQUA: Yes, we want to be questioned as well!

ISIDORO: But I've finished, d'you understand?

PASQUA: You'd better listen to us, d'you hear?

LUCIETTA: Because we know what to tell you!

ISIDORO: Women! Women! The devil take all of you!

SERGEANT (*entering right*): Sir! His Excellency the Chancellor has just arrived! (*Exit.*)

PASQUA: Ah, *he*'ll see we get justice!

LUCIETTA: That's right! We'll go and see *him*! *We*'ll go to the Chancellor!

ISIDORO: You can both go where you please! If you ask me you're all mad: the whole lot of you! Nothing but a lot of backbiting, vixenish she-devils! (*Exit left.*)

PASQUA: By heavens, he's gone too far! Oh! He's going to be sorry for speaking like that to us! When we've finished with him he'll be singing a different tune!

LUCIETTA: Yes, fancy speaking to us like that! I never heard anything like it! A man like that wants teaching how to behave!

PASQUA: And I'm just the person to do it! I'll give him a lesson or two he won't forget in a hurry. Follow me! (*Exit right, followed by* LUCIETTA.)

CURTAIN

ACT III

Scene I

A street in Venice.
As Act I, Scene I. Later the same day.

BEPPE (*entering back-stage and coming down front centre*): Oh,
what does it matter! *Let* them arrest me if they want to!
Anything would be better than skulking about like this,
hiding away from everyone! Yes, I'd even *die* content – if I
could just give Orsetta a good hiding first! As for that
Monkey-face, I'll have one of his ears off *him* – even if I'm
sent to the galleys for it! (*Looking around him.*) All the doors
are shut. Everybody must have had to go to the Chancellery. (*Voices off right.*) This sounds like somebody now.
It may be that Sergeant after me again. No! It's Orsetta!
Now's my chance to settle things with *her* – once and for
all!

LIBERA, ORSETTA *and* CHECCA *enter, right, their shawls
round their shoulders.*

LIBERA (*gently*): Beppe!

ORSETTA (*lovingly*): Oh, my darling Beppe!

BEPPE (*with rough deliberation*): Oh, go – jump in a canal!

ORSETTA: Who – what d'you mean?

LIBERA: Who are you speaking to, Beppe?

BEPPE: All of you, the whole lot of you!

CHECCA (*to* BEPPE): Well, you can go yourself – for all I
care!

ORSETTA (*to* CHECCA): Be quiet! (*To* BEPPE.) But what have *we* done to you?

BEPPE: You'll all be glad when I'm put in prison, won't you? But before that happens I'm going to—

ORSETTA: But that will never happen! You've got it all wrong!

LIBERA: Yes, Vincenzo has just told us! We needn't worry any more! Everything is going to be arranged!

CHECCA: And we've got the Commissioner on our side, as well.

ORSETTA: So you see – why be angry with *us*?

BEPPE: With *you* I can, then.

ORSETTA: With me?

BEPPE: Yes, with you.

ORSETTA: What've I done?

BEPPE: What did you have to get mixed-up with that Monkey-face for, eh? Why did he come here looking for you?

ORSETTA: For me?

BEPPE: Yes – looking for you! To speak to you!

ORSETTA: Who's told you that?

BEPPE: My sister-in-law and my sister told me.

ORSETTA: Liars!

LIBERA: Liars!

CHECCA: Oh, what liars!

ORSETTA: It was Checca he came to speak to!

LIBERA: And then he went over and sat with *your* sister.

ORSETTA: And it was to her he gave the sweetmeats!

CHECCA: And that's why Titta-Nane has quarrelled with Lucietta!

BEPPE: Titta-Nane's quarrelled with my sister? Why's he done that?

CHECCA: Because of Monkey-face.

ORSETTA: So where do I come into all this? That's what I'd like to know!

BEPPE (*to* ORSETTA): Then Monkey-face didn't come to speak to you? He spoke to Lucietta? And Titta-Nane has quarrelled with her?

ORSETTA: Yes, you pig! Haven't you any confidence in me, you – you snake! Have you no faith in your poor Orsetta, who loves you so and who worries herself to death all the time you are away from her?

BEPPE: But why did they tell me such a story?

LIBERA: Because they want to lay the blame on us – for what's all their fault.

CHECCA: Yes! And we've done nothing. They just want to cause trouble for us.

BEPPE (*threateningly*): Just let them wait till they get back here! I'll show them!

ORSETTA (*to* LIBERA): Hush! Here they are now!

LIBERA (*to* CHECCA): Quiet!

CHECCA (*to* LIBERA): But I'm not saying anything!

> LIBERA, ORSETTA *and* CHECCA *retire left, beside their door, as* PASQUA *and* LUCIETTA *enter right, their shawls over their shoulders, and come centre.*

LUCIETTA (*to* BEPPE): What is it? What's the matter?

PASQUA (*to* BEPPE): What are you doing *here*?

BEPPE (*indignantly*): What was it you were both telling me before?

LUCIETTA (*moving down front right*): Ssh! Come over here!

PASQUA (*following her and beckoning* BEPPE *to come to them*): Come over here and listen!

BEPPE (*loudly*): What are all these stories you've been making up?

LUCIETTA (*nervously*): Oh, do come – quickly.

PASQUA: Quickly – you poor boy!

BEPPE: What *is* it? What's the matter? (*He goes over to them and they stand either side of him.*)

LUCIETTA: You must go away!

PASQUA: Yes – as soon as possible!

Whilst they are speaking, the other three women remove their shawls.

BEPPE: But they've just told me that everything's going to be all right!

LUCIETTA: Don't trust *them*!

PASQUA: They want to assassinate you!

LUCIETTA: We have been to the Chancellery and he wouldn't even listen to us.

PASQUA: Oh, he saw *them* all right! But us – oh, no, we were shown the door, we were!

LUCIETTA: That Orsetta was in with the Commissioner for more than an hour.

PASQUA: They mean to have you brought in.

LUCIETTA: They're going to have you arrested!

PASQUA: You must get away – quickly – and hide!

BEPPE (*crossing to* ORSETTA, *left stage*): What is all this? Is this the way you betray people?

ORSETTA: What d'you mean?

BEPPE: Just trying to keep me here long enough for me to be arrested, were you?

ORSETTA: Who's said that?

LUCIETTA: I did. I said it.

PASQUA: And we know everything – we know all that's been happening—

LUCIETTA (*to* BEPPE): Hurry! You must go!

PASQUA (*to* BEPPE): Yes! You must run for it!

BEPPE (*to* ORSETTA): I'll see you pay for this!

CAPTAIN TONI *enters backstage and comes down centre.*

PASQUA: Oh, dear, and here's my husband now!

LUCIETTA: Brother, why have you come back!

PASQUA: You must go away!

LUCIETTA: They mustn't find you here!

TONI: Take it easy! Take it easy, there! There's no need to worry any more! Vincenzo has been to see me. He's spoken with the Chancellor, everything has been arranged, and we can come out of hiding.

>LIBERA, ORSETTA *and* CHECCA *all turn on* BEPPE *down front left.*

ORSETTA: There you are! What did I say?

LIBERA: Just what we've been telling you.

CHECCA: So we're liars, are we?

ORSETTA: Want to have you arrested, do we?

>BEPPE *strides angrily across to* LUCIETTA *and* PASQUA, *right centre.*

BEPPE: So you two have been at it again! Can't you stop making things up? What is it going to be next?

>*Enter* VINCENZO, *right.*

ORSETTA: Here's Vincenzo now! Everything *is* arranged, isn't it, Vincenzo?

VINCENZO: Nothing is arranged.

ORSETTA: But – why not?

VINCENZO: Because that blithering ass Monkey-face won't make it up with youse all – and until 'e's willing to do that, nothing can be arranged.

>PASQUA *and* LUCIETTA *turn on* TONI, *centre stage.*

PASQUA: You hear that?

LUCIETTA: Haven't we just told you?

PASQUA: Nothing's been settled?

LUCIETTA: Nothing has been arranged.

PASQUA: They mustn't find you here!

LUCIETTA: Go and hide again – at once!

>TITTA-NANE *enters left and stays moodily down front left.*

PASQUA: Titta-Nane! Oh, why have *you* come here, as well?
TITTA-NANE: That's my affair and nothing to do with
    you.
LUCIETTA: But the sergeant might find you!
TITTA-NANE (*to* LUCIETTA, *scornfully*): It would take more
    than a Sergeant to frighten me. (*To* VINCENZO.) I come
    from the Commissioner. He sent for me. He says I can
    come and go as I please and I've no need to worry myself
    over anything.
LIBERA (*to* LUCIETTA): Didn't I tell you that the Com-
    missioner is on our side?
    The SERGEANT *enters backstage and strides centre stage.*
SERGEANT: Toni Canestro, Beppe Cospettoni, and Titta-
    Nane Moletto, you are to accompany me to the Chancellery.
PASQUA: I knew it! I knew it! We'll never see you all again!
LUCIETTA: What will become of us all!
PASQUA (*to* ORSETTA): Everything arranged indeed!
LUCIETTA (*to* ORSETTA): A fine friend he's turned out to
    be – your Commissioner!
    ISIDORO *enters right and strides centre stage.*
LUCIETTA (*as she sees* ISIDORO): Huh! Speak of the devil!
ISIDORO: Well, who's going to be first?
ORSETTA: That lot over there, Illustrious. We don't know
    anything about it all.
LUCIETTA: What do you want with our men? What d'you
    want them for?
ISIDORO: Nothing, my dear, nothing at all. Just let them
    come along with me and they need have nothing to fear. I
    have been given charge of this little affair: the Chancellor is
    leaving it all in my hands. Vincenzo, will you go and find
    Toffolo and do the impossible by bringing him here? If he
    won't come willingly, however, tell him I'll have him
    brought here by force.

VINCENZO: Yes, sir! At once, sir! Beppe and Captain Toni, will you come along with me? I've something to tell you.

TONI: Of course, Vincenzo.

> TONI *and* VINCENZO *go off right*.

TITTA-NANE (*aside, down left*): They're not going to get me budging from here!

BEPPE (*to* ORSETTA): See you later, Orsetta!

ORSETTA (*to* BEPPE): You're not still angry, then?

BEPPE: Let's forget all about it! See you soon! (*He goes after* TONI *and* VINCENZO.)

ISIDORO (*aside to* CHECCA, *who has beckoned him down front right*): Yes, what is it, child?

CHECCA: Have you spoken to him?

> TITTA-NANE, *down left, watches them sullenly*.

ISIDORO: I have.

CHECCA: What does he say?

ISIDORO: To be frank – neither yes or no. But I think that the two hundred ducats would not displease him.

CHECCA: I am in your hands, Illustrious.

ISIDORO: Rely on me. (*Aloud, to* TITTA-NANE.) Well, let us go, Titta-Nane.

> TITTA-NANE *stands irresolute down left. He looks at* LUCIETTA *talking to* PASQUA *and studiously ignoring him. He looks at* CHECCA, *down right, who returns his look with a coy smile. He looks back at* LUCIETTA *and appears completely miserable*.

TITTA-NANE (*to* ISIDORO *who has turned waiting for him*): All right. I'll come.

LUCIETTA (*to* PASQUA, *as he passes them*): Not even a good-bye!

PASQUA (*to* LUCIETTA): What a lout he is?

TITTA-NANE (*turning to them disdainfully*): Your servant – ladies!

ISIDORO (*aside to* TITTA-NANE): Say good-bye to Checca!

TITTA-NANE (*with warmth*): I'll be back soon, my pretty one!

    LUCIETTA *pulls a face.*

CHECCA (*coyly, coming centre*): I'll be *waiting*, Titta-Nane! (*She rejoins* LIBERA *and* ORSETTA *left stage.*)

    ISIDORO *and* TITTA-NANE *go out right.*

LUCIETTA (*to* PASQUA): Did you hear that? My pretty one! Huh!

PASQUA: I wonder what he's up to now?

LUCIETTA: And her, as well! (*She imitates* CHECCA *loud enough for her to hear.*) I'll be *waiting*, Titta-Nane! Ooh!

CHECCA (*loudly*): Are you trying to make fun of me again?

ORSETTA: She'd do better to pull herself to bits for a change.

LIBERA: Oh, she thinks herself too good for everybody!

LUCIETTA: Yes, it would be rather hard to pull myself to bits – since I don't go round pulling other people to bits. I just wouldn't know how.

PASQUA (*to* LUCIETTA): Take no notice! You know what she's trying to do!

CHECCA: Huh! I'm sure I don't know what you're talking about.

ORSETTA (*to* LIBERA): Yes! What did she mean by that?

LIBERA: Just don't answer her back. Let's show her that some people at least have got some sense!

LUCIETTA: How wise we're getting! But girls who've got any sense don't go around stealing young men from other girls.

ORSETTA: Meaning what – for example?

LUCIETTA: Titta-Nane – for example.

CHECCA (*quickly*): Titta-Nane's finished with you!

PASQUA: Huh! Where d'you get that idea from?

LIBERA: Everybody knows he has!

PASQUA (*loudly*): You're nothing but a spiteful, lying gossip!

ORSETTA: You shut up, big mouth!

LUCIETTA: Listen to fish-face!

LIBERA (*ironically*): Listen to 'pretty one'!

LUCIETTA: Prettier than that sister of yours, anyway!

CHECCA: All this is really just beneath my contempt!

LUCIETTA: What a nasty little thing you are!

ORSETTA (*approaching* LUCIETTA *with a menacing gesture*): Say that again! Go on, just you say that again!

PASQUA (*interposing herself between them, to* ORSETTA): And who's going to give her a good hiding, eh?

ORSETTA (*dashing back into the fray*): I'll tear you to bits if you're not careful!

LUCIETTA: Oh, what a harpy!

ORSETTA (*giving her a push on the shoulder*): Are you going to stop that sort of talk?

LUCIETTA (*using both her arms to send* ORSETTA *staggering with a push*): Oh, go away and don't annoy me!

LIBERA (*giving* LUCIETTA *a push*): You just get over on to your own side of the street!

PASQUA (*giving* LIBERA *a push*): Who d'you think you're pushing?

ORSETTA (*bounding back into the fray*): I'll scratch your eyes out for that!

    The five women are all thumping each other and squealing and shrieking, when FORTUNATO *dashes out of his house.*

FORTUNATO: Stop it! Stop it, d'y hear! Stop it, you silly lot of c-cows! Stop it! Stop it!

    He dives into the middle of them and finally manages to separate them, herding his own womenfolk towards his door.

LIBERA (*as she goes into her house*): You're right! Yes, that's all they are! A silly lot of cows!

ORSETTA (*also going in*): Just you wait! I'll – I'll pull your hair out for this!

CHECCA (*also going in*): Yes, you'll all pay for this, just you see!

PASQUA (*calling after them*): If it wasn't for this rheumatism in my arm, you'd all be stretched out flat!

LUCIETTA (*to* FORTUNATO): And as for you, you old crow, if you don't thump a bit of sense into those women of yours, we'll – we'll shove your head into one of your silly big spittoons!

FORTUNATO: Go away! Go on, both of you! Women, women! Always – b-b-brawling! Always qu-quarrelling! G-get b-back into your own house b-before I start b-b-boxing your ears for you!

Quick CURTAIN *as he chases them into their house*

Scene II

A room in the Chancellery, as in Act II, Scene I.

ISIDORO (*urbanely*): So you see, Titta-Nane, that all I'm trying to do, all I want to do, is to make peace between you all, to put an end to all this tittle-tattling, and to all these brawls and squabbles which it leads to. You all understand, I'm sure, that in my position as Commissioner, I try to be the friend of you all, and especially of all you good fisher people.

TITTA-NANE (*looking round uncomfortably*): It is very kind of you, Excellency. Er – where are all the others, Illustrious?

ISIDORO (*suavely*): Vincenzo has gone to find Monkey-face and to bring him here. I've sent Captain Toni to look for my servants to ask them to have some flasks of wine ready to celebrate a grand reconciliation between you all. And as for Beppe – you see I'm hiding nothing from you – I've sent Beppe to fetch Fortunato and all the – er – all the ladies.

TITTA-NANE: But what if Monkey-face won't come?

ISIDORO (*impatiently*): Then I'll have him brought here – by force if necessary. (*Trying to recover his suave urbanity.*) However, tell me, my dear fellow – tell me – what is your reply to the proposition I made to you this morning? Does Checca please you? Would the dowry I mentioned be agreeable to you?

TITTA-NANE: To tell you the truth, she pleases me little and I wouldn't marry her with twice that dowry.

ISIDORO (*exploding*): But – that's not what you said this morning!

TITTA-NANE (*nervously*): How d'you mean – not what I said this morning?

ISIDORO (*indignantly*): You said that you weren't sure, that you wanted to know how much dowry she'd have. And I told you that she'd have two hundred ducats or more. It certainly seemed to me then that the dowry was to your liking – and it seemed to me as well that the girl herself didn't displease you. So why this sudden change of mind?

TITTA-NANE: But I haven't, Illustrious! I haven't changed my mind. You know – everybody knows – I've been courting Lucietta now for two years. Just as everybody knows how quickly I lose my temper. So you see, I did what I did just out of jealousy. Lucietta's played me a rotten trick. So I lost my temper and broke off our engagement. But I couldn't give her up altogether, Illustrious. Don't you see? It's all nigh breaking my heart, Illustrious!

ISIDORO: So! You want me to weep for you, eh? You want

me to hold your hand for you? Me, who've already told
Fortunato and Libera that I want to speak to them about
Checca's marriage!

TITTA-NANE (*miserably*): I'm sure I'm very grateful to you,
Illustrious.

ISIDORO: You don't want Checca then?

TITTA-NANE (*still more miserably*): Thank you for all your
kindness, Illustrious.

ISIDORO: Yes or no!

TITTA-NANE: With all respect to you, Illustrious – no.

ISIDORO: Then you can go and hang yourself – so long as
you don't come bothering me any more!

TITTA-NANE: There's no call to speak like that, Illustrious.
I'm a poor man, a poor fisherman, yes. But I am also a man
of honour, Illustrious!

ISIDORO: I am sorry. It is just that I would have liked to
have seen you married to Checca.

　　　VINCENZO *enters right followed by* TOFFOLO.

VINCENZO: Here I am, Illustrious. And here 'e is. Yuss, I
made up 'is mind for 'im, all right!

TOFFOLO (*bowing to* ISIDORO:) 'Lustrious!

ISIDORO (*rising and coming front left*): Come here!

TOFFOLO (*still bowing as he approaches* ISIDORO): Yes,
Illustrious! Yes, Excellency!

ISIDORO: Now just you tell me this. Just exactly what is
your reason for lodging your complaint against these three
men?

TOFFOLO: Why, because they want to kill me, Excellency!

ISIDORO: They do *not* want to kill you! They want to be
your friends!

TOFFOLO (*muttering*): Aye – so they can stab me in the back!

TITTA-NANE (*to* TOFFOLO, *menacingly*): Eh! What's that?

ISIDORO (*to* TITTA-NANE): That's enough! You be quiet!

(*To* TOFFOLO.) And you, pay attention to what I'm going to say, unless you want to find yourself in prison!

TOFFOLO: Yes, of course, Excellency!

ISIDORO: You deserve to have a complaint made against *you*, for having thrown those stones. Do you know what would happen to you if these people did make a complaint against you? I'll tell you! In view of the premeditation with which you've made a complaint against them – you would be ordered to pay heavy damages and costs.

TOFFOLO: But I'm a poor man, Excellency! I wouldn't be able to pay! (*To* VINCENZO *and to* TITTA-NANE.) Go on, then, kill me! I'm only a poor man, so have your way then and kill me!

VINCENZO (*disgustedly*): You'll say that once too often, young feller! Look, let's shake 'ands all round, and forget about it all.

TOFFOLO: But how do I know I'd be safe? (*To* ISIDORO.) What reason 'ave I got to trust them all?

ISIDORO: Very well – if that's all you want! Titta-Nane, do you give me your word not to molest him any more?

TITTA-NANE: So long as he leaves Lucietta alone, and stops hanging around her all the time.

TOFFOLO (*going down front right, jauntily now that he feels safe*): Huh! No wonder you're all mixed-up, if you think I hang around here because of Lucietta!

ISIDORO: Well, what *does* bring you around here then?

TOFFOLO: The girl I'm thinking of marrying, of course.

ISIDORO: What girl?

VINCENZO: Orsetta?

TOFFOLO: Not likely!

ISIDORO: Not Checca, surely?

TOFFOLO (*laughing loudly*): Right first time, Excellency!

TITTA-NANE (*going up to him, angrily, down left*): What a liar you are!

TOFFOLO (*excitedly*): There – he's at it again! What right's he got to call me a liar?

TITTA-NANE: Because Checca has told me, and Libera and Orsetta have told me, that it was Lucietta who you sat beside.

TOFFOLO: But I only did that just to annoy somebody!

TITTA-NANE (*belligerently*): Who? Who were you wanting to annoy?

ISIDORO (*leading* TITTA-NANE *away centre stage*): Titta-Nane, calm yourself, please! (*To* TOFFOLO.) Do you really mean what you said about Checca?

TOFFOLO: I swear I do!

ISIDORO: And you wish to marry her?

TOFFOLO: If I get the chance!

ISIDORO: And she? Would she accept you?

TOFFOLO: Why not? What reason would she have for not accepting me? I am going to have my own boat at Vigo and soon I'll be able to afford to marry.

CAPTAIN TONI *enters right followed by* SANSUGA *and* SANSOVINO *carrying flasks of wine.*

TONI: Here are your servants, Illustrious.

ISIDORO: Good! Everything is working out fine. Put down the flasks and go and get some glasses from the kitchen. (SERVANTS *exeunt left.*)

TONI (*to* VINCENZO): How are things going?

VINCENZO: Fine, fine! Everything is going to be all right!

ISIDORO: Well, Toffolo, I think we might be able to arrange this marriage for you!

TOFFOLO: Heaven will reward you, Excellency.

TONI: Marriage? Who with?

ISIDORO: With Checca.

TONI: And my brother Beppe will marry Orsetta!

ISIDORO: Excellent! And Titta-Nane will marry Lucietta!

TITTA-NANE: If she comes here of her own free will, it's possible I might.

ISIDORO: Enough of that! It's time you all made up your minds whether you're going to marry or not. I'll provide a meal as a celebration, sugar almonds, a good meal. We'll have a real party and all enjoy ourselves. (*He pours out the wine into the glasses which the servant has brought.*)

TOFFOLO (*helping himself to a glass of wine*): Happy days, Captain Toni!

TONI (*helping himself to a glass*): Happy days, Vincenzo!

VINCENZO (*also taking a glass*): Happy days!

ISIDORO: A glass for you, Titta-Nane?

TITTA-NANE (*taking a glass surlily*): This doesn't mean I've given in, you know!

ISIDORO: Drink it up, lad, and make peace.

TOFFOLO (*shaking hands with* TONI): Peace, Captain Toni!

TONI: Peace it is!

TOFFOLO (*taking* TITTA-NANE'S *hand and shaking it vigorously*): We're friends, eh?

TITTA-NANE: Ay, friends it is, I suppose.

TOFFOLO (*shaking hands with* VINCENZO): And you, Vincenzo!

VINCENZO: Friends we are indeed! All friends. Everybody's friends! Jolly good pals! (*He starts singing but is interrupted by the sudden entrance of* BEPPE, *right.* TOFFOLO *seizes* BEPPE'S *hand and starts pumping it.*)

TOFFOLO: It's peace, friend! It's peace, between us all, brother-in-law!

BEPPE (*panting, out of breath*): Stop it! Stop it! Something's happened! Be quiet, and listen while I tell you!

ISIDORO: What has happened?

BEPPE: They're all in an uproar! Scratching and screaming and pulling each other's hair out!

ISIDORO: Who are?

BEPPE: The women! All of them! I went to fetch them here, as his Excellency said! They wouldn't even let me in. Orsetta actually banged the window in my face! And Lucietta doesn't want to speak to Titta-Nane any more either! They're all shouting fit to burst. I'm afraid they'll all be fighting like cats again by now!

TITTA-NANE (*shouting*): By heavens, this is too much! A man can stand so much, but this is going too far! (*He dashes out of the room, right.*)

TONI (*muttering*): Sorry, Excellency – but I must go and defend my wife! (*He dashes out of the room, right.* VINCENZO *follows him.*)

BEPPE (*shouting at* ISIDORO): If they hurt them, you're going to have another law suit on your hands! (*He dashes out of the room.*)

TOFFOLO(*gibbering*): Oh, they won't hurt Checca, will they? They'll leave Checca alone, won't they? Oh, dear, perhaps I'd really better go and see what's happening! (*He dashes out of the room.*)

ISIDORO(*groping dazedly to his chair and collapsing*): It's true! They *do* want to drive me mad!

Quick CURTAIN

Scene III

As Act I, Scene I. Later the same day. LUCIETTA *is standing in the doorway of her house.* ORSETTA *is standing facing her opposite, in the doorway of her house. Both have their arms folded belligerently.*

PASQUA'S *voice is heard from within her house on the left.*

LUCIETTA (*calling across to* ORSETTA): What's that you say? You don't want my brother any more? Huh! As if *you* ever were good enough for him!

ORSETTA (*answering from opposite*): Well, at least I won't have much difficulty in finding somebody better than him!

LUCIETTA: Oh? Who, for example?

ORSETTA: A pig!

LUCIETTA: You can't marry a close relative like that!

ORSETTA: Why don't you try keeping your mouth shut for a change?

LUCIETTA: I would – if I had teeth like yours!

ORSETTA (*shouting*): At least I'm a respectable girl!

LUCIETTA: Fancy that! I'd never have guessed it!

ORSETTA: It's a wonder your tongue doesn't choke you!

LUCIETTA: What a spiteful cat you are!

PASQUA (*from within*): Lucietta! Come inside, Lucietta!

LUCIETTA: Things would be a lot better round here without you!

ORSETTA: Without who?

LUCIETTA: Without you.

PASQUA (*from within*): Lucietta!

ORSETTA: Sour grapes! Nobody wants you, that's your trouble! If any poor chap did marry you, he'd have a fine time, with you nagging him all day long! No wonder Titta-Nane finished with you! Couldn't stand the sound of that voice of yours any more, I expect!

LUCIETTA: It was me who broke it off with Titta-Nane, not him with me!

ORSETTA: There you are! Sour grapes! I said it was that!

LUCIETTA: I couldn't care less, especially if he's going to marry that dirty slut of a sister of yours!

ORSETTA: You watch that tongue of yours!

PASQUA (*from within*): Lucietta!

LUCIETTA: The day *I* want to get married, I'll have plenty to choose from! (*She goes in again.*)

ORSETTA (*calling after her*): Yes, you'd better go in, before I really start telling you what I think of you! (*She goes in to her house.*)

LUCIETTA (*reappearing*): Pasty-face!

ORSETTA (*reappearing*): Tittle-tattle!

LUCIETTA *imitates the sound of a sheep and goes in again.*

ORSETTA (*calling after her*): Some people have got no manners! Ignorant, that's what you are! (*She goes in again.*)

LUCIETTA (*reappearing*): And what d'you think you are – a lady?

ORSETTA (*reappearing*): Which is what you'll never be!

TITTA-NANE, TONI *and* BEPPE *enter, left.*

TITTA-NANE: Are you two still at it!

LUCIETTA: Oh, you – you go and speak to your Checca! (*She goes in.*)

ORSETTA (*to* TITTA-NANE): Don't pay any attention to her! She's going out of her mind.

TONI (*to* ORSETTA): And *I'd* say you were helping her to!

ORSETTA: *She* doesn't need any *help*!

BEPPE (*reproachfully*): Orsetta!

ORSETTA: Oh, you go and hang yourself! (*She goes in.*)

TONI (*to* TITTA-NANE): Take care not to come near our house again. I don't want to see any more of you.

BEPPE (*to* TITTA-NANE): And keep away from that house as well, you're not wanted over there either.

TITTA-NANE (*bristling*): That's enough to make me go there now, even if I hadn't any other reason!

BEPPE: If only I hadn't promised Monkey-face, I'd teach you a lesson or two! (*He goes into their house, left.*)

TITTA-NANE (*cocking a snook and calling after him*): And that
   goes for me too!

TONI: You needn't expect to come on our next voyage. So
   you'd better find yourself another boat. I'll soon find some-
   one to take your place. (*He goes into his house, left.*)

TITTA-NANE (*his temper exploding violently*): By heavens!
   Somebody's going to pay for this!

   VINCENZO *enters right.*

VINCENZO: Well, Titta-Nane, 'ow are things going?

TITTA-NANE (*bellowing*): A dagger! Give me a dagger!

VINCENZO: A dagger? Have yer gone mad? What's the
   matter with yer?

TITTA-NANE (*misery and fury making him appear almost in-
   articulate*): I'll hang if I have to, but by heaven, I'll stretch
   three or four of them first!

   TOFFOLO *enters right, still quite happy and on top of the
   world.*

TOFFOLO: Here I am! What's going on?

TITTA-NANE (*going up to* TOFFOLO): A dagger! Quick! A
   dagger!

TOFFOLO (*screaming*): He's at it again! Stop him! Stop him,
   somebody! Stop him!

   TOFFOLO *starts running off, right, but collides violently with
   ISIDORO. ISIDORO gives him a push and sends him flying to
   the ground. ISIDORO is accompanied by his SERVANT.*

ISIDORO: Fool! Idiot! Imbecile!

TOFFOLO (*still screaming*): Help! Murder! Help!

ISIDORO: What's the matter with you? Get up!

TOFFOLO (*getting up, but keeping an eye on* TITTA-NANE): It
   was him! He tried to kill me!

ISIDORO: Who did?

TOFFOLO: Titta-Nane there!

TITTA-NANE: He's a liar! I said before, he's a liar.

ISIDORO (*to* TITTA-NANE): Get away from here! And be
quick about it!

VINCENZO (*with ill-advised patience*): No, no, you've got it
wrong, Illustrious. It's not 'im 'e's after, Illustrious. It's
Beppe and Captain Toni. It's them he wants to do in.

ISIDORO (*to* VINCENZO: *everything once more becoming too
much for him*): He's not doing *anybody* in while I'm around!
(*To* TITTA-NANE.) Get yourself out of here! Did you hear
me?

VINCENZO (*to* TITTA-NANE): Come on, lad. You'd best
do what his Excellency says, eh?

ISIDORO (*trying to regain control of himself*): Yes, you take him
away, Vincenzo. Keep him with you. Stay under the
arcade in the piazza. If I need you I'll send for you.

VINCENZO: Yes, Excellency. (*To* TITTA-NANE.) Let's go,
old chap.

TITTA-NANE: No, I don't want to.

VINCENZO: Now, there ain't nothing to worry about any
more. You'll see. Just you come along with me and forget
all about it.

ISIDORO: That's right. You go along with Vincenzo. Just
leave everything to me and I'll see that you get the satis-
faction you deserve.

   TITTA-NANE'S *fury has subsided under the kindness ap-
parent in their voices, leaving him pathetic in his proud misery.*

TITTA-NANE: I'm obliged to you, Illustrious. I'm only a
poor man, but I'm a man of honour, you know, Excellency. (VINCENZO *begins leading him off.*) I am obliged to
you, Illustrious – your Excellency – his Excellency the
Commissioner—

   (*Exit left*).

ISIDORO: Come here, Toffolo!

TOFFOLO: 'Lustrious?

ISIDORO: Do you want us to speak to the girl and see if she's agreeable to marrying you?

TOFFOLO: Heaven will reward you, Illustrious, but perhaps first it would be better to speak to her sister Libera, and her brother-in-law, Fortunato.

ISIDORO: All right, then, if they're at home.

TOFFOLO: Should I call them?

ISIDORO: No, no, we might as well just walk in.

TOFFOLO: Oh, but *I* can't go into their house!

ISIDORO: Why ever not?

TOFFOLO (*reproachfully and self-righteously*): In Venice, Illustrious, young men do not visit the house of a respectable young lady without the permission of the young lady's father or guardian.

ISIDORO (*sarcastically*): But it's in Venice, isn't it, that *you* spend most of your time talking to these respectable young ladies?

TOFFOLO: In the street, Illustrious, in the street. It's only when we've spoken to a young lady's father about marriage that we can visit her in her house.

ISIDORO: All right, all right, call them, then! Call them!

TOFFOLO (*calling*): Ho, there! Fortunato! Donna Libera!

LIBERA *comes out of her house, right.*

ISIDORO (*aside, down left*): It's that deaf one again! She'll drive me mad!

LIBERA: What is it? What d'you want?

TOFFOLO: Here is his Excellency, the Commissioner.

LIBERA (*curtseying to* ISIDORO): Your servant, Illustrious!

ISIDORO: I thought you were deaf!

LIBERA: Oh, no, Illustrious. I did have a little ear-ache, but it's better now, thank you.

ISIDORO (*suspiciously*): It's got better very quickly, hasn't it?

LIBERA: Oh, it comes and goes, you know, Illustrious!

ISIDORO (*glaring at her*): Yes, it comes no doubt *very* con-
veniently when you . . .

>*He is interrupted by* FORTUNATO *who comes dashing out of
his house with his shirt half-way on.*

FORTUNATO: 'Lustrious!

ISIDORO: Oh well, now you're both here, I suppose I'd
better tell you what I wanted to see you about. I want to
know if you'll be agreeable to a marriage I've arranged for
Checca.

LIBERA: Heaven will reward you, Illustrious. It'll be a
pleasure to lose her!

FORTUNATO: I've p-p-promised her a hundred d-d-ducats,
'Lustrious.

LIBERA: And there's another fifty we've saved up.

ISIDORO: And I will add another fifty!

LIBERA: Heaven bless you, Illustrious! And the young
man? You haven't told us who he is yet!

ISIDORO(*pointing to* TOFFOLO): Well, how does this young
man here please you, eh?

FORTUNATO (*gibbering with indignation*): A j-joke, eh! You
m-make f-fun of us, eh? T-Toffo the M-monk! That
howling t-t-tom-cat! He look for another qu-quarrel,
eh?

TOFFOLO(*sententiously*): *I* don't pick a quarrel with anybody
so long as they leave me alone.

LIBERA: But how can *he* support a wife?

TOFFOLO: I'm going to buy a boat, aren't I?

LIBERA: Well, where'll you take her? You won't even have
a roof over your head!

FORTUNATO: P-p'raps he thinks they'd live in his b-boat!

TOFFOLO: You *could* keep your hundred ducats, of course,
and give us a room with you.

ISIDORO: An excellent idea! He's got more sense than I

thought. You would only have to put them up for a short
time.

LIBERA: How short, Illustrious?

ISIDORO (*to* TOFFOLO): How long d'you think? For a
hundred ducats?

TOFFOLO: Well, I don't know . . . six years, at least, I'd say.

FORTUNATO: Why n-not say sixty while you're at it!

ISIDORO: But it really wouldn't be at all a bad arrangement
with a little economy all round.

TOFFOLO: You decide then, Illustrious.

ISIDORO: Well, what about a year? Would you agree to
that?

TOFFOLO (*sententiously*): I'll be agreeable to whatever you
decide, Illustrious.

ISIDORO (*to* LIBERA): Call the girl, and let us see what *she*
has to say.

LIBERA (*calling into the house*): Checca! Checca!

FORTUNATO (*bawling at the top of his voice*): Checca! Checca!
CHECCA *comes out very quickly.*

CHECCA: Here I am! Do you want me?

LIBERA: Yes, as if you didn't know!

CHECCA: Well, I couldn't help overhearing you all. Really,
I couldn't!

FORTUNATO: Spying little nosey-parker! What d'ye mean –
you couldn't help it?

ISIDORO: Never mind, never mind! (*To* CHECCA.) Well,
what do you say then?

CHECCA (*to* ISIDORO): Can I say what I like?

ISIDORO: Yes, that's what I'm here for – to protect your
interests, my child.

(*He and* CHECCA *go down-stage, left.*

CHECCA (*aside to* ISIDORO): What about Titta-Nane? Isn't
there any hope?

ISIDORO (*aside to* CHECCA): No, I'm afraid there isn't, my
  dear.

TOFFOLO (*aside, to* FORTUNATO): What's the idea –
  whispering to him like this?

CHECCA (*aside to* ISIDORO): But why?

ISIDORO (*aside, to* CHECCA): Because he still loves Lucietta.

TOFFOLO (*coming centre*): Your Excellency the Commissioner!

ISIDORO: Yes, what is it?

TOFFOLO: I would like to hear what's going on, as well.

ISIDORO (*to* CHECCA): Come then! Make your mind up.
  Do you want him or *don't* you?

CHECCA (*to* LIBERA): What d'you say, sister? (*To* FOR-
  TUNATO.) What d'you think, brother-in-law?

LIBERA (*to* CHECCA): What d'you say yourself? *D'you* want
  him?

CHECCA: Why not?

TOFFOLO (*jubilantly*): She's accepted me! Did you hear?
  She's accepted me!

ISIDORO (*leads* CHECCA *across to* TOFFOLO, *right centre*):
  Yes, yes. So you needn't waste my time any more. You and
  Checca, at any rate, are off my hands. You'd better marry
  her as soon as possible.

  ORSETTA *comes out of the house right, having obviously been
  eavesdropping.*

ORSETTA: What's that? Checca getting married before *me*?
  But *she's* six years younger than me! She's got no right to
  be married before me!

FORTUNATO (*to* ISIDORO): Yes, that's true, Illustrious.

CHECCA (*to* ORSETTA): You're only jealous! Get married
  yourself then, if that's how you feel. Nobody's stopping
  you, I'm sure!

FORTUNATO (*to* ORSETTA): Yes, that's true. If you want

to get married so much, why then get m-married – or else keep your m-mouth shut!

LIBERA (*to* ORSETTA): Yes, you *had* a young man yourself. But *you* had to go and quarrel with him!

FORTUNATO: Yes! Always qu-quarrelling!

ISIDORO (*to* LIBERA): Wasn't Beppe her young man?

LIBERA: Yes, sir – Beppe!

FORTUNATO (*bellowing*): B-Beppe it was, sir!

ISIDORO: One moment. (*He goes to the door of* BEPPE'S *house, right, and calls.*) Beppe, are you at home?

   BEPPE *appears immediately.*

BEPPE: Here I am, Illustrious!

ISIDORO: Why have you quarrelled with Orsetta?

BEPPE: Me, Illustrious? But it's the other way round; she won't have any more to do with me!

ISIDORO (*to* ORSETTA): Well, miss?

ORSETTA: Oh, well, you know how it is – one says things and then one's sorry afterwards.

ISIDORO (*to* BEPPE): Well, sir?

BEPPE: It's the same with me – I'm a little quick-tempered myself and then . . .

ISIDORO: Good – then this is another affair settled! (*To* ORSETTA.) You don't want Checca married before you, is that it? All right, then give Beppe your hand at once. . . .

   LUCIETTA *dashes out of her house, right; also having obviously been eavesdropping.*

LUCIETTA (*to* BEPPE): How dare you think of marrying that girl after all she's been saying about me!

ORSETTA (*angily*, *to* LUCIETTA): What's it got to do with you who he marries?

LIBERA (*to* ORSETTA): Now don't you start that all over again!

FORTUNATO: That's enough! Qu-quarrelling again! No more! You hear! No more qu-quarrelling!

BEPPE: Oh, I don't know what to say! I just want to get married!

LUCIETTA: I'm the one who should marry first! No sister-in-law's going to come into our house while I'm still there!

ISIDORO (*to* BEPPE): Why don't you get her married off?

BEPPE: Because she and Titta-Nane have quarrelled.

ISIDORO: Toffolo! Come over here! Go to the arcade in the Piazza and tell Vincenzo to come here and bring Titta-Nane with him – at once!

TOFFOLO: Yes, 'Lustrious! I'll be back, Checca! I'll be back! (*Exit right.*)

ISIDORO: Now then, what about it? Is it really quite impossible for you all to get on together and live in peace?

LUCIETTA: That depends on them over there!

ISIDORO (*to* LIBERA, ORSETTA *and* CHECCA): Well – what do *you* say?

ORSETTA: As far as I'm concerned, I couldn't care less!

LIBERA: And as for me, I'm ready to be friends with anyone, so long as they don't start pushing me around!

ISIDORO: What about you, Checca?

CHECCA: Heavens, *I* only want to live in peace with people!

ISIDORO: Well, what are you waiting for! Kiss and be friends and no more quarrelling!

ORSETTA: Well, I'm willing.

LUCIETTA: Me also!

    As the two girls embrace, PASQUA *comes out of her house, right.*

PASQUA (*seizing* LUCIETTA *by the arm and pulling her back*): And just what d'you think you're doing? Making it up with *her*? With *that* crowd?

ISIDORO (*to* PASQUA): So you're still out to cause trouble, are you?

PASQUA (*still to* LUCIETTA): I can't make you out! I really just can't make you out! After all the things they've been saying about us!

ISIDORO: Will you shut up, you silly woman!

PASQUA (*turning on him*): I won't shut up! Why should I, with these rheumatics in my arm fair crippling me!

ORSETTA (*aside*): *I'd* cripple her, all right.

CAPTAIN TONI *comes out of his house, right.*

ISIDORO: Captain Toni!

TONI: Illustrious?

ISIDORO: If you don't knock some sense into that wife of yours—

TONI: Enough said, Illustrious! I understand you! (*To* PASQUA.) Make your peace with them!

PASQUA: No!

TONI (*bellowing*): Do as I say. Make peace with them!

PASQUA: I won't, I won't, I won't! So there!

TONI (*beginning to take off his belt*): Make peace, d'you hear me!

PASQUA: Yes, yes, of course! If that's really how you want it – then I'll make peace of course.

ISIDORO: What a man! Well done! Well done!

LIBERA: So, Pasqua, it's peace, is it?

PASQUA: Peace it is, Libera! (*They embrace.*)

LIBERA: And the others as well! (*She embraces* LUCIETTA, *and* PASQUA *embraces* ORSETTA *and* CHECCA.)

ISIDORO: Excellent, excellent! So this squabble is over and peace is made (*aside*) until they're at it again!

VINCENZO, TITTA-NANE *and* TOFFOLO *enter, right.*

VINCENZO: Here we are, Illustrious!

ISIDORO: Ah! Titta-Nane! Come over here please, will you? (TITTA-NANE *goes over and stands beside him docilely.*) Well,

Titta-Nane, it's high time that you realized I'm only out to help you – and that you started showing yourself to be a man.

VINCENZO: That's just what I've been telling 'im, Excellency. And, to tell you the truth, I think 'e's beginning to see that your Excellency knows what's best for 'im.

ISIDORO: So? Then we'll let bygones be bygones! Come, make it up with everybody, and get ready to marry Lucietta!

TITTA-NANE: No, Excellency, I'm sorry – but I'll be damned if I will. (*He goes and stands obstinately down front left.*)

ISIDORO (*wildly*): Excellent! Oh, that's perfect! That just makes everything perfect! (*He stamps pettishly back stage away from them.*)

LUCIETTA (*aside*): Oh, I could – *thump* him!

PASQUA (*to* TITTA-NANE): Listen, you big cod fish! If you're thinking of trying it on with Checca, you can think again! She's already engaged to be married to Toffolo.

FORTUNATO: Aye, that's right! And I'm g-g-giving them a hundred d-ducats!

TITTA-NANE: Checca! Just what are you getting at now! She can marry who she pleases, for all I care!

ISIDORO (*returning centre stage to* TITTA-NANE): The question is – why don't *you* want to marry Lucietta?

TITTA-NANE: Because she said I could go to the devil. That's what she said! Those were her very words!

LUCIETTA: Well, I like that, I must say! I suppose you never said anything to me? Oh, no!

ISIDORO: All right! All right! That's enough! Even if *he* can't make up his mind, thank heaven other people can! Checca and Toffolo, give each other your hand.

TOFFOLO: Here am I.

CHECCA: And here am I. (*They stand together in front of* ISIDORO.)

ORSETTA(*pushing them aside*): Oh, no, you don't! I should be married first, not you!

ISIDORO (*vehemently*): Heaven give me patience! Beppe! Forward!

BEPPE (*coming forward self-consciously to* ISIDORO): Well, here goes! I'd best get it over with, I suppose.

LUCIETTA (*pushing him aside*): Oh, no, you don't! I'm not being married, then you're not either!

PASQUA: I think Lucietta's right!

TONI (*to* PASQUA): Are you starting again? What's it got to do with you? You just ask what *I* think first in future!

ISIDORO: If you ask *me* what I think, I'll tell you! (*Shouting.*) You can all go to the devil! I am absolutely and completely fed up with the whole lot of you!

> He stamps angrily backstage left, and sits with his head in his hands on the bench against the house, left. The whole cast turn to him, so that he sits at the apex of the triangle of which they all compose the two sides. They continue pleading, each repeating their line, as follows, until he rises and comes forward centre again, i.e., after he has counted up to about ten.

CHECCA (*to* ISIDORO): But, Illustrious, you promised me!

FORTUNATO (*to* ISIDORO): 'Lustrious!

ORSETTA (*to* ISIDORO): You can't leave us now!

FORTUNATO (*to* ISIDORO): 'Lustrious!

LIBERA (*to* ISIDORO): Just have a little more patience, Illustrious!

ISIDORO (*returning front centre: to* LUCIETTA): Because of you, we're all back where we were at the beginning!

LUCIETTA: You've no call to talk like that, Excellency! I don't want to have caused any trouble. But if I have, it's me that's getting the worst of it! Titta-Nane doesn't want me

any more – all right, I'm not complaining! But after all,
what did I do to him? Even if I did speak foolishly, the
things he said to me were far worse! And if I'm willing to
forgive him, surely he should be willing to forgive me? It
just shows he doesn't want me any more! (*She begins to weep*.)

PASQUA (*with warm compassion*): Lucietta!

ORSETTA (*to* TITTA-NANE, *who is still down front left*): Now
look what you've done!

LIBERA (*to* TITTA-NANE): She's crying!

CHECCA (*to* TITTA-NANE): It's all your fault!

TITTA-NANE (*aside, miserably, as the others flock commiserating
round* LUCIETTA): As if I didn't know it!

LIBERA (*to* TITTA-NANE): Have you no feelings at all? Just
look at the poor child! It's enough to move a heart of stone!

TITTA-NANE (*going up to* LUCIETTA, *right centre, brusquely*):
What is it you want, then?

LUCIETTA (*weeping*): Nothing.

TITTA-NANE (*to* LUCIETTA): Come on! It's not as bad as
all that, is it?

LUCIETTA: What's it got to do with you?

TITTA-NANE: Well, what's all this snivelling about then?

LUCIETTA (*flaring up*): Oh, you beast! That's all you are! A
cruel beast!

TITTA-NANE (*imperiously*): Be quiet!

LUCIETTA (*miserably but proudly*): All right. I know you
don't want me. I'll go. (*She starts moving left*.)

TITTA-NANE (*going and blocking her way*): Do you want to
drive me daft?

LUCIETTA (*sobbing*): No!

TITTA-NANE: Well, d'you want to marry me then?

LUCIETTA (*still sobbing*): Yes!

TITTA-NANE: Captain Toni, Donna Pasqua, Illustrious,
with your permission (*to* LUCIETTA) give me your hand!

LUCIETTA (*giving him her hand*): There!

TITTA-NANE (*still brusquely*): So – now you're my wife!

ISIDORO: Splendid! Excellent! (*To his servant.*) Sansuga!

SANSUGA: Illustrious!

ISIDORO: Go quickly and do as I told you to!

SANSUGA: At once, Excellency! (*Exit right. During the following lines he and* SANSOVINO *bring in wine and trays of sweetmeats and place them on the two benches against the houses.*)

ISIDORO: Now, you, Beppe! It's your turn next!

BEPPE: All ready and waiting, Illustrious! Fortunato, Donna Libera, with your permission! (*He takes* ORSETTA'S *hand.*) Husband and wife!

ISIDORO: Well, Toffolo? Who's next?

TOFFOLO: Aye, it's me, Excellency! Fortunato, Donna Libera, with your permission! (*He offers his hand to* CHECCA.)

CHECCA (*to* ISIDORO): Wait! What about the dowry?

ISIDORO: I have given my word. You may rely on me.

CHECCA (*to* TOFFOLO): Here is my hand, then!

TOFFOLO: My wife!

CHECCA: Husband!

TOFFOLO: Happy days, everybody!

FORTUNATO: Happy days! (*To* LIBERA.) It t-takes me back to the day you g-gave me your hand, my love!

LIBERA: Now don't you start trying to be funny.

SANSUGA (*to* ISIDORO): Everything is ready, Illustrious, as you commanded.

ISIDORO: Husbands and wives! I have had a little refreshment prepared. Some musicians are ready also. We will celebrate with eating and drinking and dancing!

LUCIETTA: Illustrious! Before we dance and celebrate, may I say just one little thing? I shall never be able to thank you for what you have done for me. And I am sure the others all say the same. But, please, Illustrious, when you leave us and go back to your fine friends, do not let them think that the fisherfolk of Venice are for ever squabbling and brawling! (*She turns and addresses the audience.*) For what you have seen and heard has all been but as chance would have it. We fisherwomen of Venice are good women, respectable women, but we live joyously and passionately. We would like to go on doing so. And we would like you to say to all: '*They* know how to *live*, the fisherfolk of Venice!' Long live the fisherfolk of Venice!

ALL: Long live the fisherfolk of Venice!

Quick CURTAIN